CountryLiving

SALVAGE STYLE

Decorate with Vintage Finds

Leslie Linsley

HEARST
books

HEARSTBOOKS

An Imprint of Sterling Publishing Co., Inc.
1166 Avenue of the Americas
New York, NY 10036

ISBN 978-1-58816-928-0

Distributed in Canada by Sterling Publishing
c/o Canadian Manda Group, 664 Annette Street
Toronto, Ontario, Canada M6S 2C8
Distributed in Australia by NewSouth Books
45 Beach Street, Coogee, NSW 2034, Australia

For information about custom editions, special sales, and premium and corporate purchases,
please contact Sterling Special Sales at 800-805-5489 or specialsales@sterlingpublishing.com.

Manufactured in China

2 4 6 8 10 9 7 5 3 1

www.sterlingpublishing.com

Design by woolypear

CONTENTS

The bifold doors on a guest cottage were crafted out of old windows, and the vintage iron pendants were redesigned with paper shades and wire lampshade frames.

INTRODUCTION

All my life I have been attracted to "junk."

My heart does flip-flops whenever I pass a junkyard, and I scour my local newspaper every week for the yard sale. When I'm on a road trip I will gladly take a detour if I pass a sign announcing a flea market "just up the road and around a bend." I admit to being a die-hard salvage junkie. Because I live on Nantucket, a historic island off the coast of Massachusetts, I am surrounded by some of the earliest homes in this country. I like to furnish my house with pieces that come from these homes, and for that reason, I spend a lot of time at local auctions. We have a saying: "Nothing good ever leaves the island; it just gets recycled in someone else's home."

I have always had a garage or basement full of other people's discards in the belief that they will reveal their decorating worthiness in due time. Eventually they do, and I become a bit smug, congratulating myself on my astuteness for having recognized a good buy when I found it. And you will too! No matter where you live in this country, you can find great salvaged materials or furnishings to repurpose to create an interesting home. And I've added a guide on page 154 to help you get started.

What is salvage style? Before it became a style of remodeling or decorating a home, recycling materials like barn wood and architectural pieces from dismantled early homes and industrial buildings was merely a sign of frugality. But over the years the use of an old barn door in a modern home, installing old beams on a modern kitchen ceiling, or mounting industrial wheels to a piece of weathered wood to create an interesting coffee table became chic. Homeowners and decorators began to recognize these one-of-a-kind touches for what they were—a way to infuse a home with old-fashioned character. Deep-rooted respect for the past is often a motivating factor for salvage devotees. They enjoy having something in their homes that can transport them to a gentler time.

In this section I've included lots of general tips on salvage style and how-to-do-it directions. Throughout the book you'll find real life examples of how homeowners in all parts of the country creatively incorporated salvage style into their homes.

Mix and Match

Decorating with scrap materials has become a chic approach to making a room, or even an entire house, fashionable, interesting, and unique. Reclaiming local, honest materials that tell a story of their heritage has become very appealing when building or renovating a house. Collectible items from the past represent an easy way to infuse a home, no matter when it was built or in what style, with the warmth and charm associated with everyday items from the past. For example, when a collection of early cooking implements is displayed on shelves made from recycled, weathered materials, it immediately elevates a kitchen from everyday to extraordinary. Worn items are comforting to live with and provide an unexpected aesthetic.

Two twin-sized salvaged wood headboards are paired to create an interesting statement. The adjoining master bath is connected by way of large barn doors on a track.

A 1900 cottage was purchased fully furnished, but the homeowners saved only the pieces with potential, like the sage cupboard and painted pine dining table surrounded by new chairs. The cushions on the window seat are reminiscent of early patterns.

Where to Find It

Simply recognizing these items as "valuable" has opened up whole new businesses, and salvage or junkyards have become regular haunts for new homeowners. Outlets for finding things to reclaim, renovate, restore, and repurpose from the past are everywhere. Flea markets, thrift shops, antique stores, swap meets, yard sales, and secondhand stores abound. Online sites for salvaged goods, from appliances to hardware, proliferate, and it is now possible for anyone to find almost anything, from the mundane to the unusual, anywhere in the country. In fact, if it's the look you're after, but you want up-to-date function, as in the case of appliances, you can easily find something that looks old but functions like new. Many companies offer reproductions of well-designed, retro items whose designs have stood the test of time.

Depending on where you live, the salvaged material that is available will vary. For example, when a young couple from Tennessee saw a barn being demolished, they were compelled to liberate a few roof beams and doors. They like foraging for salvaged materials in their area, so when a pair of hand-forged iron hooks caught their eye, they grabbed them, even though, at that moment, they didn't have a use for them. Collectors have a knack for spotting salvaged material with potential. *Advice:* If it looks good and the price is right, grab it when the opportunity arises. Eventually you'll find a use for whatever it is and congratulate yourself for being so intuitive.

When you first decide that using salvaged material for remodeling or decorating is a good idea, you may not know exactly where to start. In fact, you may not be sure of what you want. However, it won't take long to become immersed in the world of salvage devotees, and the learning curve is fun. After all, who doesn't love a treasure hunt? And this is what it's all about—hunting for treasures from the past. Learning to recognize the well designed among what is simply junk comes with practice. However, in the hands of a creative person, that piece of junk can often be turned into a showpiece.

COUNTRY ICONS include such items as grain sacks; hand-painted signs; wicker furniture; wooden tool caddies; cast-iron tubs, doorknobs, and hinges; vintage linens and quilts; grain scoops; and antique pine benches and trunks, all with potential for recycling—not always in their original state.

When it comes to a collection of vintage vases, a collector says, "There is always some shape, size, color that has escaped me. The origin is unimportant. Nothing beats the thrill of the hunt."

Salvage yards provide the perfect hunting grounds for finding treasures among the detritus of everyday life from the past. For example, one homeowner who grew up scouring flea markets with his thrifty parents now fills his home with found objects. "I have an eye for what's good, and I can pretty much guess what it's worth." He advises, "If you aren't sure about price, don't pay more than your budget allows, unless you absolutely can't live without it. You don't want to have buyer's remorse."

Bargain Hunting

When it comes to searching for salvage, an experienced hunter has this advice to impart: "It's a cliché, but the early bird really does catch the worm. My parents were so poor when I was born that they raided my great-grandfather's shed for furniture. Living with passé American oak dressers and other hand-me-downs gave them an appreciation for cast-offs, many of which have since come back in vogue, like industrial lamps and factory stools." Often, being on a budget forces you to find things to repurpose. **Beware:** Once you begin, it can become an obsession, but a happy obsession—one that can be a lot of fun.

VINTAGE DOORKNOBS

can be found in salvage yards, or go online for reproductions. Preservation Station (thepreservationstation.com) is one source.

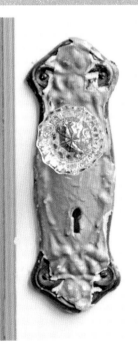

Salvaged material sparks ideas for creative decorating. And if you don't consider yourself particularly creative, ideas from homeowners, sprinkled throughout the book, about what they found and how they used it to transform a room, along with photographs of the finished projects, will give you hundreds of ideas for your own home. Once you tune in to salvage style, you'll find yourself looking at discarded items with new eyes wherever you go. Everything has potential if you're looking. It's out there. With a little practice, you'll see it.

Start small. For example, a bathroom can be transformed with the use of unconventional fixtures or an ornate chandelier from the Victorian era. It's the unexpected that gives a room that "wow" factor. A deep porcelain farmhouse-style sink adds old-world charm to a modern kitchen, as will a collection of mismatched vintage chinaware or baskets clustered together on open shelves. The provenance of a collection is unimportant. Mirrors and wall décor can be created from salvaged picture frames (hardware stores will cut mirrors to fit) and the use of bar stools made from tractor seats at a high-tech kitchen island gives the room that wonderful contrast, like combining a little chocolate with vanilla ice cream.

A FEW "RULES" FOR BARGAIN HUNTING

* Hit your favorite shopping haunts on a regular basis. You'll get to know the owners, who might teach you a thing or two and learn about your tastes. You'll also see what isn't selling, which will help you bag a deal.

* Rather than trying to wear dealers down, make one bid. If something is marked twenty dollars, for example, offer fifteen. If they say "no," leave it at that. Then you can decide if you want the item badly enough to meet the asking price.

* Learn how to use Craigslist to your best advantage. For example, go beyond the obvious keywords (kitchen island) to include, say, "industrial" or "school" or "factory."

A modern kitchen retains its country charm with butcher-block countertops, shelves from salvaged wood and reclaimed wooden brackets painted white, metal and wood industrial-style stools, and iron and glass lighting fixtures. Old wooden floorboards and ceiling boards are painted white. Cabinet drawer pulls give a nod to the past. Faucets and sink are pure farmhouse style.

A deep cast-iron claw-foot tub was purchased at a junkyard and then refinished to provide character in a bathroom where the pitched ceilings made a standard-height shower a no-go.

Garden trellises were painted soft seafoam green and repurposed as twin headboards. Small mirrors were mounted on each one.

Kitchen cabinets are painted black to match the range and topped with soapstone counters. The brass drawer pulls are very retro looking, and a secondhand brass desk lamp provides cozy lighting.

Vintage Flooring

One of the most sought-after salvage materials is wide-planked flooring with a distressed finish. It's a classic item and can become an essential element for creating a room with old-world character. It's possible to find salvaged flooring, but you can also buy flooring that has been produced to look old.

A refreshing take on old flooring is oak that is stained a dark color. It makes a dramatic statement in an all-white or pastel environment. A patina from wear and tear will develop over time, making the floor look even better.

Another material often repurposed is old brick. One homeowner salvaged a chimney, installed radiant heat in the kitchen floor, and covered it with the old bricks. It's always toasty warm.

Wide floorboards were left natural, but the shiplap walls were painted white. This modern farmhouse has a clean, rustic feel. The furnishings are a mix of raw wood and industrial materials. The antique wooden filly, nearly 6 feet wide, makes a modern, graphic statement.

Antique Beams and Barn Wood

Reclaimed beams and barn wood, as well as barn doors and rustic wood siding, are desirable for repurposing in a new home—they add great texture and a patina of age. Barn wood is also used to make furniture such as a dining table or for creating a kitchen island. Antique red barn wood siding and weathered barn board reclaimed with all its peeling paint, nail holes, cracks, and splits are ripe for creative uses. These items are easy to find on eBay, and the prices, like the items, vary greatly.

Tin Ceilings

Originating in the 1880s as an affordable way to dress up "the fifth wall," tin was not only aesthetic but also meant to emulate high-end decorative plaster. It also offered a measure of fire prevention during a time when cooking was done with an open flame. Four-foot panels were originally stamped out of steel and called steel ceilings. It wasn't until later that the raw steel panels were plated in tin to help slow down rusting. Today, most panels are made of 30-gauge tin-plated steel and a mere $1/100$-inch thick. Many historic patterns are still sold seventy years after tin's heyday came to an end. But now you have a wider choice of factory finishes and more do-it-yourself-friendly ways to install the panels. (Etsy and eBay are good sources for these.)

Cast-Iron Planters

Once used as estate planters, cast-iron urns are highly sought after because they are unexpected and unusually interesting for use in outdoor gardens, to flank a front door, and as interesting vintage accessories indoors as well. However, while the originals are becoming scarce, many companies make reproductions, cracks and peeling included, to look just like the originals. It's almost impossible to tell the difference. It isn't difficult to find replicas of circa late 1800s styles and medium-sized vessels to punctuate your home and gardens with a touch of old-world elegance.

RECLAIMED WOOD

When you use reclaimed wood for any part of a home improvement or remodeling project, you're giving old wood new life. Perfectly good older wood comes with a story. Reclaimed wood comes from shipping and crating materials, deconstructed buildings, old gym bleachers, and wine casks, to name just a few sources.

*An antique door with its original mint
paint, found through a renovation firm,
adds interest to a modern house.*

CHAPTER 1

Kitchens

A Hoosier cabinet is filled with mismatched chinaware accumulated at tag sales
and flea markets along with a mix of whiteware platters.

When it comes to decorating, building, or renovating, most of us know exactly what we want — modern appliances. We want them to be up-to-date and function optimally. However, even a modern kitchen can benefit from a few salvage details to make this room unique. It is possible to retrofit salvaged wood over the fronts of appliances, like a refrigerator, for example, to blend in with the rest of a room that has been designed in retro fashion.

Since we spend a great deal of time in the kitchen, creating an interesting environment that is top-notch functional makes a lot of sense. Some of the ways to do this are with salvaged lumber on the walls, wide pine boards used for flooring, stone, and industrial-style accessories or furniture like old bar stools, a weathered bench or shelving, lighting fixtures, storage bins, and repurposed retro appliances.

Another material that gives a nod to a bygone era is stainless steel. Inspired by industrial kitchens, this stain-proof surface is durable and versatile, with a gutsy look. Restaurant castoffs offer a great source for a kitchen with flavor. Look for oversized commercial signs for punctuation on walls.

If you don't want to replace old kitchen cabinets, removing the cabinet doors and painting the outside and interiors with contrasting paint colors is the easiest and fastest way to transform your space. Some homeowners have lined their cabinets with retro wallpaper for a dramatic statement.

Hunting and Gathering

Finding salvaged materials to create a special kitchen can be most satisfying. One approach is to design your idea of the perfect room, down to the last detail and then look for materials and items you imagine will work with your plan. Ideas can come from many sources: books, magazines, online sites, or a combination of the best features from your friends' kitchens. Your salvage-designed kitchen might begin with interesting wood floorboards, old beams on the ceiling, a vintage appliance, or one great find like an old door around which you build the look. Another way to furnish your kitchen is to let the design evolve, one piece at a time, as you find it. If you have an open mind, you're more likely to find some interesting and unexpected things at good prices. Sometimes uncovering great stuff really cheap is part of the excitement and an ultimately great reward when your kitchen project is finished. You can enjoy your well-earned bragging rights when your friends *ooh* and *ahh* over your out-of-the-ordinary kitchen. Something to keep in mind when choosing appliances, consider the resale of your home. Even a vintage kitchen can benefit from modern appliances.

Take advantage of hallway space and create a mudroom with salvaged door frames (check out the rope balls used for hooks)
and a bench crafted from reclaimed barn wood.

Remodeling

Whether you're remodeling a kitchen in an old house or infusing a newer kitchen with the kind of style that comes from salvaged material, you might want to start from the ground up. If the floorboards are wide planks or otherwise interesting but flawed, rather than replacing them, consider stripping the old finish and either painting or staining the exposed clean wood.

A wood-covered ceiling and heavy beams will give the most modern kitchen a warm farmhouse feeling. For an interesting contemporary-meets-retro look, consider using new lighting, such as a mix of large dome pendants and swing-arm lamps, in a rustic space. Make an island with reclaimed wood for the top secured to two old sawhorses also made from reclaimed wood.

If your kitchen ceiling is low, upper cabinets will feel clunky, especially if you've installed large beams. In this case, open shelving is preferable. Use weathered wood to make exact sizes needed to fit specific areas. Found brackets add interest, but pairing worn wood with modern hardware can provide an unexpected and good-looking contrast.

A homeowner restored the kitchen in his 1700s stone house, paying tribute to its past while adding a few modern-day upgrades.

A sleek modern kitchen retains its roots with the original wood flooring, ceiling boards, and old beams. Cabinets with blue-gray undertones balance the warmer hues of the original wood.

A cramped, blank, no-personality kitchen was renovated with still-functioning industrial pulleys, once used in a billiard hall, for eye-catching (and hardworking) task lighting above the island.

The kitchen is the first room homeowners are most likely to renovate. They are also most definite about what they want in that room and how they want it to function. This usually depends on the makeup of the family and their lifestyle. Those who entertain casually, for example, might forfeit a formal dining room for a big family-style kitchen. Family and friends seem to be drawn to gathering in the kitchen, and this room often functions for more than preparing meals.

Remodeling a kitchen in an older home often involves enlarging it by forfeiting a dining room or stealing space from an existing hallway. It's an opportunity to use salvaged material with modern amenities to maintain the charm and intimacy of the original small room while upgrading it with modern conveniences.

How to Begin

Before you start, make a list of everything you love about your old kitchen, including how it feels to be in it. Then, make a wish list for improvements. Take photographs of every detail to refer to when away from home and looking for material. Creating a design scrapbook is a good idea. Every time you see a picture you like in a magazine, cut it out and paste it into your book. Take pictures of details you like in your friends' kitchens. Go on house tours whenever possible. Real estate agents often have open house tours when selling houses. It's an opportunity to see what others have done.

Collect paint color swatches and ideas for details like cabinet knobs, lighting fixtures, wood colors for cabinets, appliances, and furniture. Pick up free design brochures in home centers and paint stores.

One couple spent two decades in their 1930s California home before making the decision to tackle the renovation of their kitchen. They enlarged the space by taking down a wall and combining it with the formal dining room, and then updated it with fresh takes on vintage country style. They managed to keep the original yellow-and-red color scheme that they loved so much. Now the kitchen is the center of their social scene, from book club meetings to dinner parties. It has become the hub of the house.

Look Beyond the Façade

When a young woman went looking for a house in Long Island, New York, her first reaction to the rundown bungalow she was shown was "No way!" But the price and location were too good to turn down. The house was dark and had low ceilings, so the first thing she did was cover the walls with white-painted beadboard. Paint is the easiest and cheapest thing you can do to create a working canvas. She then extended the backsplash of kitchen tile up to the ceiling for a dramatic effect. The ceramic tiles' concave centers and a milky white glaze add an old-world texture that stands out next to the sleek new appliances. Another easy first step when transforming a space is to switch out run-of-the-mill lighting for instant wow appeal.

IT'S ALL IN THE DETAILS

1. A sunny, upbeat yellow paint color on kitchen walls can be charming. *Caution:* Yellow is a tricky color. Try using a paint color two or three shades lighter than the color swatch you like, and try it out in a small area before committing to the final color.

2. Pale mint green is a retro color for granite countertops.

3. Bright accents of red—for example, on the range hood, metal chairs, and knobs—perk up the kitchen.

4. Red-striped schoolhouse glass lighting shades are a nod to the 1930s. Look for them on eBay or Etsy.

5. Without a formal dining room, a large wooden table serves all purposes. If you can't find the perfect size weathered table, use salvaged wood to create a tabletop that's just right. Make it the centerpiece of the room.

6. It's easy to make café curtains from vintage napkins. Almost every yard sale and secondhand shop has an abundance of linens to use for this project. Even if white linens are yellowed or stained, they can be reclaimed with soap, water, and bleach.

7. An open shelf over the sink window can hold early canisters and mixing bowls or other useful collectibles in your color and design scheme.

8. For a farmhouse-style detail, line glass-front cabinets with chicken wire.

9. Arched toe kicks under cabinets give standard cabinetry a one-of-a-kind vintage feel.

Salvaged hardware, like the cherry knobs on the kitchen drawers, adds old-fashioned charm to new furniture. The large farm-style table is more serviceable than an island for this family's needs. All meals from formal to casual are served here.

Instead of overhead lighting, picture lights illuminate an art collection as well as stove and countertop workspace. Painted white planks on the walls and a reclaimed beam give the kitchen a farmhouse feeling. Fresh green herbs in galvanized paint buckets flank the black fireclay sink.

A couple with two young sons transformed a cheerless 1970s ranch house into a warm and cozy farmhouse using white-planked walls, a soothing blue-and-green palette, and architectural details, fixtures, and finishes. It was easy to combine two rooms to make one open living space. Once they'd reconfigured the layout, the small rooms were no longer dark and choppy but rather open and bright. They added a reclaimed rough-hewn beam to the kitchen ceiling, swapped plate glass windows and doors for those with divided light, replaced the sporadically placed veneer paneling, and installed oak hardwood flooring everywhere. "It's a way less suburban, more authentic, rural farmhouse now," they say. All in all, it was an inexpensive remake created with a little salvaged and repurposed material.

Sometimes a trip to another part of the country or overseas can inspire a different approach to decorating or remodeling at home. After a trip to Paris, a couple from the Midwest outfitted their kitchen with classic white subway tiles, polished marble, and copper accents reminiscent of their favorite French bistros. A pine ceiling gave the kitchen a country vibe, and painting the room an inky black upped the space's cool factor and created a focal point at the center of the home. "I've always loved shiplap and other wood panel finishes," the homeowner said. "But it wasn't in our budget to use those materials throughout the entire home, so we just did a ceiling or wall here and there." This is a good way to compromise and get what you want.

The antique copper ship lights were salvaged from a Florida dockyard. Silver cordial glasses passed down from a great-grandmother decorate the fireplace mantel, and soda-shop stools from the 1940s were found at an antique shop.

Modern Country

Is there such a thing as modern country? Having spent a decade traveling for work, one city dweller found a 1,700-square-foot log cabin in the mountains. From exterior updates to a complete interior overhaul, he tore apart his mountain retreat and then put it back together again, modern country style. By using new appliances and countertops in the kitchen and recycling much of the original material, he was able to achieve this look, which is an eclectic mix of salvaged items with contemporary materials. For example, he used a new version of country plaid and homespun fabrics in more contemporary colors like black and gray.

"Painting the walls, ceiling, and floors white really lightened things up," he said. "Installing 8-foot windows and French doors helped bring the sunlight into what was a very dark space," he added. He created the style he wanted with butcher-block countertops, black cabinetry, large industrial pendant lights, and a porcelain apron sink. Black appliances (less expensive than stainless ones) match the cabinets for a seamless effect. If a home is dark, it is often easy to transform it into a light, bright space by replacing windows, and finding salvaged windows and doors is all the better when it comes to adding both light and character.

Minimal or no window treatments is a typical modern farmhouse aesthetic. There are many small ways to introduce old-fashioned character in a modern setting. Potted herbs on the sills are all that's needed for a window over the sink. To create the look, combine traditional antiques with metal factory finds like lighting fixtures. Sandstone countertops paired with butcher block on an island are practical and good-looking materials. Rather than wood stain or white cabinets, think seafoam green for contrast. Create storage for everyday china in a freestanding armoire. Don't overlook drawer pulls and hardware. These items can make a powerful statement. Either choose all the same or vary them. Reproductions abound.

Wood floors, ceiling, and walls painted all white lightened up the kitchen. Crisp black-and-white plaid play up the preppy, country feel that the owner was after.

This kitchen's 1940s Wedgewood stove is outfitted with a custom hood, and the new fridge exudes a similar vintage vibe. Offsetting the white appliances are soapstone counters and backsplashes, as well as ash cabinetry painted a muted gray-green.

Appliances, Sinks, Stoves, and Refrigerators

Old fixtures and appliances may have the look you want for your kitchen, but they may not function as efficiently as new ones. Some companies sell reproductions that look exactly like the originals but are brand new. If you score an early appliance, consider using it for storage or display. Or, with some research, you might find someone to restore it to working order.

Soapstone is a good-looking and practical material for countertops. This material was used at the turn of the eighteenth century. It might be paired with oversized porcelain sinks instead of the more modern granite and stainless steel combo.

Deep porcelain drop-in farmhouse sinks can be found in salvage yards, but they're also available as reproductions, and copies of original faucets can be found. Pair the sink with plain wood cabinets or paint existing old cabinets white for a simple way to upgrade a kitchen with early charm. Combine all-white chinaware and serving platters with wooden bowls, cutting boards, Mason jars, utensils, and other retro items that are useful as well as decorative. Always add a green plant, pots of herbs, and fresh fruit to liven up an all-white kitchen.

This 1932 Magic Chef, with six burners and two ovens, was found at a salvage yard and brought back to life. The owners feel lucky to have found it.

This down-home space proves there's nothing cold or boring about white on white. Notice the complementary shapes and sizes of all the items on the shelves.

Farmhouse staples, from pine shelves to grain-sack linens, never go out of style. An island workspace can be created from all sorts of weathered materials or found objects. One couple stumbled on an early nineteenth-century French baker's table and turned it into the center island workspace. It totally makes the kitchen. Other staples include pine shiplap siding and cedar ceiling beams for instant aging. To brighten the room without taking away from the retro look, give the walls a coat of gray-white chalk paint.

An English pine hutch—with drawer storage below and cupboard above—stands in for traditional cabinetry. Separating the pieces created more workspace in between. Skirted panels are made from an old linen tablecloth.

Washboards

Known as "the poor man's instrument," early American washboards are in great demand for decorative accessories and as wall art. The flat board with a ribbed surface was believed to have originated in Scandinavia around the end of the eighteenth century. The first washboard manufactured in the United States has markings that, it is believed, could be from the pre–Civil War era. All washboards made today have poplar wood frames with galvanized metal, stainless steel, brass, or glass. The Amish and some Mennonite communities, who disdain electricity, still do their washing by hand with a washboard. A good source for a huge variety of name-brand washboards is the Scott Antique Markets in Ohio and Georgia.

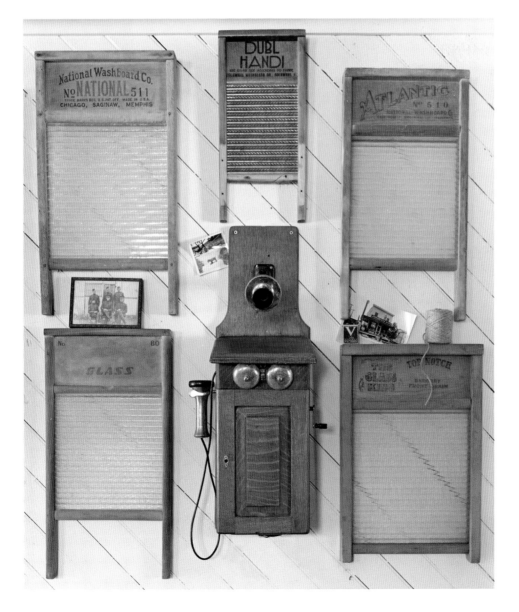

Antique washboards, picked up at flea markets for around twenty-five dollars apiece, surround a turn-of-the-century telephone that still works! The wall is covered with reclaimed boards painted white and applied horizontally.

37

EIGHT WAYS TO ADD FARMHOUSE STYLE TO YOUR KITCHEN

Some of the elements associated with farmhouse style are reclaimed wood, antique furnishings, and vintage fixtures.

1 A cast-iron potbellied wood-burning stove set on a stone slab adds charm and warmth to the kitchen. The stove doesn't have to be old. Many companies, such as Vermont Castings, make reproductions of early stoves.

2 Light woods, like scrubbed pine or oak, are associated with farmhouse style. Hang oak or pine shelves, or a glass-front cabinet, to hold ironstone pottery, creamware, or banded mixing bowls often found in early farmhouse kitchens.

3 The walls and ceilings of early farmhouses were often constructed from interlocking wood planks. Painted white, they offer a fresh, modern approach with a nod to the past.

4 Industrial-looking aged bronze lighting fixtures offer an opportunity for good-looking and functional detail.

5 A good source for retro appliances is eBay. However, many top-of-the-line manufacturers are now producing copies of early designs with state-of-the-art functions. *NOTE: If you buy a retro appliance online, be prepared to pay hefty shipping charges. Try to buy locally for this reason.*

6 Create practical and stylish storage with baskets and vintage galvanized tin boxes. Great for storing dry goods or bulky cookware.

7 Bluestone on the floors is good-looking, and combined with radiant heating, it is warm to the touch. Poured and polished cement is another interesting floor material, as are wide pine floorboards left worn in places, or sanded and stained or painted.

8 Antique doors and hardware are easy to find in salvage outlets and flea markets all over the country. They can be just the right touch if you want to add detail with character to a modern kitchen. An architectural detail salvaged from an old building can also be used as wall décor.

Farmhouse elements often include a deep porcelain sink, light wood such as oak or scrubbed pine, painted white beadboard walls, stone flooring, and industrial lighting fixtures.

Even if you live in a city apartment, it's possible to make your kitchen look like one you'd find in a country farmhouse. A woman who owns a home goods store in Minneapolis has a farmhouse-style loft above the store. Her kitchen island was constructed from packing crate slats. "I love older things that once had another purpose," she says. "They have personality, character, and soul."

A 1950s worktable and clamp-on lamp from a flea market, a metal sign from a 1920s trolley car, and a 1970s industrial Wolf range from Craigslist combine to give this kitchen personality—all for a song.

OAKLAND

An industrial worktable topped with custom-cut glass serves as the kitchen's island; the stools were rescued from a factory. A vintage zinc icebox offers hidden storage, while open Douglas fir shelves hold dishes and cookware. The stainless steel stove is manufactured by Jenn-Air.

Beadboard

A common millwork product, it is milled with a tongue on one side and a groove on the other to make an integrated surface like strip flooring. It comes in various sizes and thicknesses. Historically, beadboard was a basic, slightly decorative finish for wall coverings in kitchens, back halls, stores, and porch ceilings. It caught on as a material to use in summer cottages. It can be applied vertically or horizontally on walls or ceilings. Occasionally, it has been put up on the diagonal. The beauty of beadboard is its versatility.

White Ironstone

A popular and much sought-after collectible, this china was first made in Staffordshire, England, in 1813. It was harder than earthenware and stronger than porcelain. In 1842, the first white ironstone china was marketed to Americans. In the late 1850s and 1860s, ironstone was decorated with wheat, prairie flowers, and corn motifs to appeal to farmers. It was sold in large quantities in agricultural communities across the country.

Inside this convincingly "old" heart pine icebox are all the modern conveniences of a Sub-Zero fridge.

Stoneware bowls collected at flea markets and yard sales hold home-grown vegetables and herbs.

Yellowware

For an antique look in a country kitchen, turn to stoneware. This is the category into which various types of yellowware fit. Yellowware is defined by the color of the clay used. A clear glaze is then applied. The color varies from pale yellow to butterscotch to a bright yellow, depending on the clay. Yellowware was produced in England and Scotland as early as the sixteenth century and around 1840 in America. It is still being produced today. Yellowware is mostly found in the form of mixing bowls in all sizes. They are lovely to display on kitchen shelves or in a salvaged cupboard, as they are durable and practical as well as good-looking. Any time you have a collection of things that don't just sit on a shelf looking pretty but also can be used for everyday purposes, it adds to the enjoyment and appreciation of the collectibles.

A breakfast nook houses a rustic cabinet perked up with a new coat of paint and filled with yellowware bowls. Decorative paper transforms plain white shades to pick up the yellow colors in the bowls and vintage wallpaper.

A small eating area barely provides room for the oak table, two mismatched chairs, and a high chair. There is just enough room to pull the table out from the wall to add a chair at each end when needed.

Tables and Chairs

If you have room in your kitchen for an eating area, the table and chairs will be an important factor in your décor. Size and shape are important. Measure your area and know if you will be more comfortable with a round, oval, square, or rectangular table. If the space is small, you might consider a drop-leaf table or one that can be extended with an inset leaf for the occasional times when you need to seat more. However, be sure you have the space, even if temporary, to squeeze in a few more.

Warming up a modern or all-white kitchen is easy to do with wooden shelving or furniture. For example, open shelves made from salvaged wood always express a retro feeling. A work island and counter stools will also do the trick. Of course, wooden floors go a long way toward this end as well.

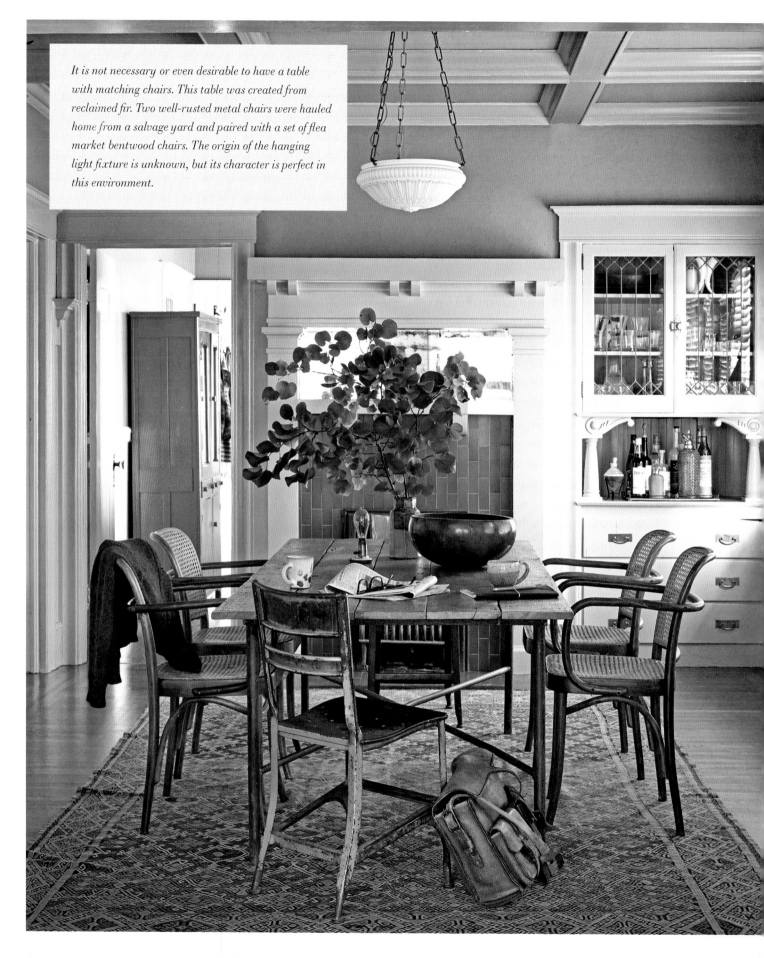

It is not necessary or even desirable to have a table with matching chairs. This table was created from reclaimed fir. Two well-rusted metal chairs were hauled home from a salvage yard and paired with a set of flea market bentwood chairs. The origin of the hanging light fixture is unknown, but its character is perfect in this environment.

Found at a flea market, a wood and metal military desk–turned–prep island is the star of the room. The weathered wood top and rusty green base give the all-white kitchen personality. Barn wood shelves echo the warmth of the island's counter.

A map pennant banner picks up the colors of the metal chairs and is the perfect trim on a salvaged door attached to the end wall of a dining area. Vintage science lab charts add color and interest to an all-white wall.

Most scavenger hunters agree that when you find something you love, always buy it, because you'll find a way to make it work. It may not come to you right away, but eventually you will find a way if you love it. While on a scavenger hunt, with nothing particular in mind, a couple felt they hit the jackpot. They found not only a wonderful farm table and brightly colored metal chairs, but also an Oriental rug that was in great shape. "When we put it all together, the eating end of the kitchen looked a bit hodge-podge," they said. "But then we found a giant, scuffed-up pocket door in an old warehouse. We snatched it up instantly, not really knowing where it would go." It turned out to be perfect at the end of the room and established the layered-over-time vibe that makes the dining area look cool and collected.

Clever cabinetry: this barn-like door is the ultimate two-for-one. It hides unsightly appliances, like a waffle maker and deep fryer, and boasts a chalkboard inset panel for keeping track of grocery lists. The door hardware can be found online.

GROCERY LIST:

COFFEE
JELLY
MILK
cake flour
ARUGULA
QUINOA
cereal
almonds
KALE
paper towels

Create a Custom Workspace

If you have sufficient space, you can create an expansive 12-foot-long work surface from two identical 6-foot-long tables. The tables serve as the base and one piece of salvaged wood sits on top to unify them. Vintage bar stools and factory lighting fixtures will complete this work area.

Plank-front cabinets and hand-forged iron strap hinges were popular in Colonial times. If you choose this route, consider buttermilk for your paint color. Other Colonial colors include barn red, deep green, and muddy blue.

The 12-foot-long workspace doubles as the perfect place to serve casual meals. Plank-front cabinetry is inspired from Colonial times, as are the paint colors on the furniture and walls.

Be Creative

Finding new ways to use ordinary items can offer exciting possibilities. For example, find inventive uses for utilitarian antique items, like clamp-on factory lamps that can be used to illuminate a worktable. An old bureau might work for holding table linens in the kitchen. Consider painting it or replacing drawer pulls if necessary. Putting two pieces together, such as a cupboard on top of a bureau to create a serving bar, is clever and practical. It's not unlikely that you will stumble on a piece of furniture that isn't perfect as is, but when paired with something else, even open shelves above the bureau, it can work.

A collection is always more interesting when you have a lot of one thing. It makes a definite statement. It might be ironstone pitchers and serving dishes, or everyday mixing bowls. Arrange them in a salvaged cupboard. Or mix and match vintage china patterns. Thrift shops are good resources for chinaware.

Little things can make a big impact. Many kitchens lead to a back door and sometimes include a hall or doorway where coats and boots are removed. Treat this area as you would any room in the house, rather than an extension of the kitchen. Look at it from a practical, as well as aesthetic, point of view. For example, if the area is small, look for an interesting clothes tree to hold coats, an umbrella stand, and a weathered bench. An industrial stool or wall hooks, a rusted planter, or a utility shelf above a row of hooks will do the trick. Vintage signs add a graphic touch.

The farmhouse cupboard dates to around 1910 and was painted red in the 1970s. It's perfect for a pure-white collection of ironware bowls and serving platters. Your local Salvation Army is a good source for finding chinaware.

This 1930s factory stool retains its original green paint.
The iron hooks on this coatrack swivel from side to side.
The wood was cut from an old locker-room unit.

A variety of collectibles, from blue Mason jars to a tackle
box, line the mudroom's ledge.

Reclaimed wood is so much more interesting than new lumber for shelves. It's easy to cut it to the exact sizes you need for any kitchen wall. The trick to making it work is the brackets. This kind of hardware seems to be readily available; you're likely to stumble upon them in most salvage yards. Finding just the ones that appeal to you will be worth the effort.

Warm up the feeling in an all-white kitchen with the use of wooden accessories, a farmhouse table, and Mexican tile on the floor. Using open shelves can be a responsibility as well as an opportunity. The shelves represent a way to arrange everyday items in a pleasing way as part of the décor, but requires you keeping things neat at all times. It's good to know how you like to live before committing to open shelves versus cabinets for storage. Using the kitchen shelves for adding salvage style is an opportunity to find little inexpensive items that appeal to you. Every time you go salvaging, you can concentrate on zeroing in on these items. It's easier than always thinking of the bigger picture because you've narrowed down the search.

If your ceilings are high, adding salvaged beams will instantly transform your kitchen. Other details will also add character. For example, a salvaged stained glass window might be used on either an outside wall or set into an interior wall to bring in light. Barn doors installed on a hinge have become the latest trend for creating more interest than new, rather plain doors. Other characteristic touches of salvage style are red tractor seats that have been reclaimed and repurposed into swiveling bar stools. Work islands might have been a countertop from a general store in another life. Ordinary objects like rustic, handmade toolboxes or grain scoops have creative uses for holding mixing tools, mail, dry goods, and other easily accessible countertop items.

A metal awning from an antique shop conceals an unattractive oven vent. The chunky, dark wooden shelves and Victorian brackets add to a modern kitchen. Inexpensive items like the retro scale on the shelf and a wooden holder for condiments on the counter are "just right" accessories.

This kitchen's circa 1900 draper's table came from an antique shop, and the cabinet fronts are made of beadboard. Reclaimed shelves were cut to fit wall to wall and add a warm color, while providing convenient access to everyday china and glassware.

Kitchen Collectibles

Collections that serve a purpose are ideal for kitchens. (You don't want to take up precious room with things that require a lot of care and don't necessarily have practical uses.) Wall art, signs, and such are the exception because they add aesthetic charm without taking up space. One homeowner filled every surface of her home with collections that included weathered accessories, antique linens, white pottery, vintage enamelware, and early wooden spoons.

THINGS TO USE AND DISPLAY

Small appliances like a blender or hand mixer, as well as wedding flatware, early cookbooks, antique silverware, wooden spoons and bowls, small aluminum tea balls, wood strawberry baskets, measuring cups, vintage cookie presses, nutmeg graters, blue Mason jars, antique wire soap dishes, metal canisters, old-fashioned colanders, wall-mounted wood spice racks, Bakelite-handled silver servers, wooden recipe boxes, vintage teapots, and candy tins—to name a few.

Enamelware and porcelain share shelf space with old maple breadboards made in the Loire Valley in France.

Concrete countertops are good-looking and durable. Barn wood left over from flooring covers a metal stove hood, and an assortment of old stools provides quirky charm.

Metal milking cans sit under a weathered table that's used as a workstation and kitchen island.

Collectibles as Art

What farmhouse would be complete without a collection of cow tags? Developed in 1799, a cow or ear tag is a metal object used for identification of domestic livestock and other animals. They were made in flag shapes and button shapes, and from plastic and metal. The first tags were made of tin. Collectors of these items use them as all sorts of decoration. Other unusual collectibles to hang on the wall might include vintage ceramic plates, game boards, early commercial signs, framed vintage advertisements, different size mirrors, and black and white framed photographs.

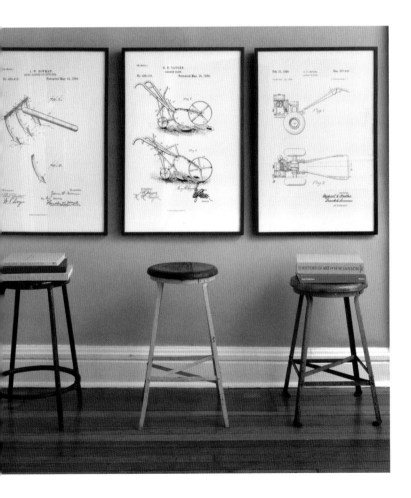

Inventive wall art can cost less than five dollars. Patents for all kinds of fascinating innovations, such as these vintage garden tools, are available for free at google.com/patents. Download images to a USB drive and have a copy shop print them on large-scale paper for framing. Wood and metal school stools are from an auction house.

A beadboard wall in a farmhouse kitchen is filled with the owner's collection of cow tags. Colorful and graphic, they are 3 inches tall. They have pastoral appeal and date to around the 1970s.

White oak shelves house a collection of old French liqueur bottles. Vintage globes represent another interesting collectible.

Old Glass Bottles

There is nothing as appealing as a beautifully shaped bottle. Old glass bottles are interesting for display. Their colors, sizes, and shapes vary greatly. They are light, delicate, and interesting when grouped together or with other objects. Many collectors look for bottles that were created to commemorate something or have some historical significance.

A sliding door provides a display area between a hallway and kitchen. Ironstone and milk pottery are from estate sales and antique stores. A good source for a modern take on white servingware is White Forest Pottery (whiteforestpottery.com).

Stoneware

A staple for storing food in many nineteenth- and twentieth-century homes, the pieces were made in the shapes of crocks, jugs, jars, and other household items. Because of its insulating properties, stoneware keeps items cool, but it can also handle heat. For this reason, it is a practical vintage item that is good-looking in any modern-day kitchen.

Breadboxes

Before refrigerators and commercially baked goods, the breadbox was essential to protect bread and other baked goods from mice and insects. A proper breadbox will have a metal interior and tight-fitting door or lid. The most interesting are white metal boxes from the 1920s with colorful trim and lettering on the front. The different typefaces, from elaborate script to stenciled letters, that spell out BREAD make each one unique.

A narrow kitchen wall is perfect for open shelving cut to size and used to display ironware pitchers and a vintage metal breadbox that is chipped and undeniably sweet.

A salvaged worktable provides the kitchen's
prep surface and reflects the color of the
turquoise-painted wood on floors and walls.
The breadbox houses the silverware. A shelf of
ironware pitchers lines a reclaimed shelf that
was painted white.

Mason Jars

Fruit canning jars are practical vintage items that display easily. The first Mason jars, as we think of them today, were produced in the 1800s. Some collectors try to accumulate as many jars as they can; pints, quarts, and half-gallons, in colors that range from standard clear, aquamarine, and green to less-common amber. Others try to acquire jars with various types of logos on their fronts.

Storage

Open shelves, an armoire, and a chest of drawers are some of the items often used for storage in farmhouse- and cottage-style kitchens. Even a modern kitchen can benefit from creative uses for furniture not originally intended for the kitchen.

To convert an armoire into a kitchen pantry, the homeowner added extra shelves and magnetic door closures.

In this mudroom, an early 1900s birdcage sits atop a vintage mailroom filing cabinet. The cabinet gives the room an industrial flavor, and the wooden school chair is good for putting on boots. A basket is handy for holding mittens and scarves or other odds and ends.

Vintage Hardware

Any piece of furniture can be made more interesting with vintage hardware. Even brand-new kitchen cabinets can benefit from antique drawer pulls and hinges. These details are the easiest way to turn ordinary into extraordinary.

Midcentury hardware from the 1950s–1970s has become quite popular for decorative trim on modern cabinets. People are looking for sturdy and durable good-looking hardware from the last midcentury. These items are very affordable and easy to find.

Other retro hardware is **French provincial** from the seventeenth and eighteenth centuries—the kind that graced the wood-carved furniture of that period. Made of bronze or copper, it is recognized by its flared leaf pattern.

Hepplewhite/Sheraton hardware style started in the late 1700s, but continued to be used and copied for generations. This hardware, like the furniture, is delicate and graceful. The hardware is oval or round with a subdued, classic design of rope trim or floral patterns.

Vintage tea towels are stacked in an old metal laundry basket.

Colorful glass insulators rest on a timeless wooden shelf.

Mission hardware is from the Arts and Crafts era of the late 1800s to early 1900s. The simple design was created in England as an alternative to the gaudy and elaborate Victorian décor. It is simple, plain, and boxy with a classy look.

Vintage Aprons

For pioneer women managing the household chores on a farm, aprons were used to carry in fruits and vegetables from the garden, eggs from the henhouse, and logs from the woodpile. The apron was also used as a potholder in the kitchen, a dust rag, an all-purpose towel for wiping flour from hands or for drying a crying child's tears. The apron was also a flag to signal to the farmhands that dinner was ready. And a shy child could easily hide behind her mother's apron. In the 1930s and 1940s, apron patterns were often printed on bags of flour or feed. All this history behind one little cloth garment adds a lot more than decoration to a modern-day kitchen. Vintage aprons can still be versatile when repurposed into pillow covers or cafe kitchen curtains. They provide a charming variety of colors and often dainty patterns reminiscent of the past.

Insulators

Insulators were designed to keep the wires linking telegraphs and telephones insulated atop wooden poles. The peak of production was in the 1920s. Commonly made from glass or porcelain in an array of shapes and colors, these are now prized by collectors for their rarity and beauty. They are exquisite objects to display on a shelf or outside on a fence. The colors include amber, cobalt blue, olive green, and royal purple.

A plywood framework and skirt made from burlap hide utilitarian pots and pans. Track lighting takes up little space but can illuminate an entire room.

CHAPTER 2

Living and Dining Rooms

White paint covers the dark knotty pine on the walls, but the ceiling is left as is in this dining nook. The aluminum pendant once lit an airplane hangar. A settee is covered with U.S. mail bags.

If you're about to start a renovation project on an old house, you might be surprised at what you find. For example, one couple discovered that much of the old materials found during their renovation could be easily refurbished for an up-to-date look. They removed a dropped ceiling and drywall in their dining room and discovered dramatic roof beams and charming beadboard underneath. Sanding and staining the old pine floors a rich ebony color brought them back to a warm glow.

Imperfect floorboards, such as those with uneven coloration, knots, different widths, often have a worn patina that you don't see in new homes. In fact, many of the building materials used 100 years ago are more interesting and often made of better quality and craftsmanship than what we find today. Even if you have a new home, using materials from the past when redesigning, renovating, or decorating your dining or living room will create that coveted lived-in look. Things from the past have a backstory that contributes to an unusual and valuable quality in a room.

We all have different tastes. So, it makes sense that there's no one definition of the "right" way to decorate a living or dining room. Input from those who have created comfortable, interesting, and well-designed rooms is always helpful in defining and achieving a style that appeals to you. Homeowners with a hands-on approach to renovating and decorating are passionate advocates for instilling homes with personality through architectural salvage details and vintage bargains.

A gardener rehabbed a 150-year-old barn, repurposing and restoring as much of the original material as possible, like the beadboard used to create window seats. No white walls here! He used a riot of color, inspired by colors in the garden to brighten up the small dining area.

Salvage doesn't have to be confined to the indoors. This reclaimed pine table, repainted wicker chairs, and oversized lantern set under a wisteria-covered pergola create a romantic outdoor dining room.

A Connecticut homeowner designed a new sunroom to look like it was added during the nineteenth century, using old bricks, stone, and barn wood on the walls. The windows were salvaged, but the chandelier is new. The wooden fold-up chair was a great vintage find.

Cabin Fever

A couple from Georgia wanted to live in a log cabin but couldn't find one. So they contacted a company that scours the country for falling down and soon-to-be-demolished structures and then works with the owners to salvage the logs, barn wood, beams, and anything else they can repurpose into newly built homes—filling them with age, character, and charm. From ceiling beams to 300-year-old heart pine floors, the cabin was made of reclaimed materials. The owner says, "This home has roots throughout the south. Each time we look at these logs we see something different."

In between the beams, the owner painted the ceiling, made of new wood. With so much natural wood, she wanted to create a visual break. This treatment is carried throughout the house. A worn painted bench is a throwback to her childhood when "there was always a bench for the kids," she says.

By taking dark color and clutter out of the equation, a traditional Massachusetts cabin is cast in a modern light. Wood-paneled walls were painted white and never looked so fresh. A folk art bench serves as a coffee table—great repurposing!

Pine walls in a 1960s ranch house were hand pickled. The bentwood rocker is from the 1970s, and a tin B was part of a gas station sign.

A breakfast nook becomes a dining room in a small house. Weathered oak benches provide seating at a vintage oak florist's table topped with zinc. The cast-iron chandelier is circa 1920s.

An Ohio couple accidentally found a sweet log cabin while trolling the Internet for a modern home. After a quick tour, they knew they'd found the perfect getaway, only 80 miles from their home. "It needed a lot of work," she says. "Planks of knotty pine covered every single wall and the ceiling of the cabin. The rooms cried out for paint, warmth, and character, but I left select areas like the bannister and ceilings as is for contrast." Knowing what to do and how far to go can be learned with trial and error. If you find yourself in a similar situation, it's always good to move slowly. Tackle one room—even one wall or floor—at a time. Live with what you do for a while before moving on. In this way, you won't be doing and redoing or, worse, regretting the hard work you put into the project. People who have had to work on a tight budget often say it was a blessing because it forced them to make good decisions.

Once the white, slipcovered sofas were in place, it was easy to add personality and warmth from wooden accessories like the coffee table and chair and from a collection of cast-off suitcases on shelves that act as good-looking and practical storage.

Tin Signs

Prior to the popularity of porcelain enamel coatings, tin signs hit their peak in the 1920s. While they were cheaper to produce, they also rusted. Today, these graphic signs make wonderful artifacts for hanging on walls in any room—rust and all.

Common tin signs include ones that read ROOMS TO LET for hotels and those advertising products.

Fishing Lures and Decoys

Wooden fishing lures are desirable as collectible items to display, especially if fishing is a passion. These were first made commercially in the late 1800s. Up until then, they were hand carved. Antique and vintage decoys are also desirable. Fishermen cut holes in the ice and used the decoy to draw fish close enough to spear. The most sought-after decoys are those made by carvers Harry Seymour and Yock Meldrum.

An industrial shelving unit is used to display folded quilt pieces, a vintage metal star, Indian clubs, a wooden duck decoy, old books and sign, brass candlesticks, and a variety of found objects.

TRANSFERWARE

In the 1700s, the emerging middle class desired an affordable alternative to delicate hand-painted tableware. Pottery factories in Staffordshire, England, responded with transferware (think Spode and Wedgewood). By the end of the century, thousands of mass-produced pieces were getting their signature ornate look by "transferring" a printed pattern from a copper plate to a special paper and then to the earthenware.

Elements of French and American country style blend together in an Arizona home. The built-in sectional has custom box cushions for seating in the living room. The oak beams were imported from France. "It's every-day-living comfortable," says the homeowner.

Solving Problems

Not every room in a house is easy to work with. Sometimes spaces can be oddly configured. For example, one homeowner had a slanted fireplace that cut into one corner of the dining room, resulting in an awkward, not-quite-rectangular layout. To restore balance, the owner flanked the window with two identical 8-foot-tall cupboards and lined the table with coordinating rugs. "When you walk in," she says, "you immediately look toward those cabinets and everything seems right." The oversized table, made of maple planks, anchors the room and offers another distraction.

Many homes today are not big enough to include a formal dining room. Early homes with small rooms are being gutted to create more informal open floor plans. With this reconstruction, the dining room is often eliminated in favor of a dining area in the kitchen. But this doesn't mean that an eat-in kitchen can't have some of the comfortable and elegant features of a dining room. For example, when selecting furniture, choose chairs that are upholstered rather than typically spare kitchen chairs. Choose a table that fits the space and your lifestyle. An all-white kitchen with dark countertops and dark stained wood floor, for example, might suggest a dark wood table surrounded by dining chairs with washable white slipcovers.

Trunks

Known as traveling or steamer trunks, these antiques were originally used as luggage for long stagecoach, train, or steamship rides. Today, many people use these trunks as furniture. They are handy for storing bulky items like blankets, linens, serving trays, and so on where space is limited. The interior is often made of wood and lined with decorative papers. A flat-top trunk, unlike one that has a domed lid, is perfect as an end or coffee table.

Restaurant supply stores offer gutsy-looking and extremely functional items to repurpose in your home—and not just the kitchen. The galvanized restaurant cart is perfect for storage in a small living room. An early trunk is a good-looking coffee table with storage for linens. Silver trophy cups are exceptionally elegant as vases, and the two salvaged sofas were reupholstered with soft, affordable blue Oxford cloth. 81

A family in upstate New York packed their home with all the things they love, from an old mahogany table to vintage black-and-white and sepia portraits on the dining room walls. They make no apologies for their many collections, believing that more is more. Oversized platters—some old, some new—are stored and displayed in a floor-to-ceiling unit. The trick to keeping this sort of collection fresh and appealing is to stick to all white with a few silver or pewter objects, like trays, for balance. White is right regardless of provenance because ivory dishes always look good enough to be displayed out in the open. It encourages guests to serve themselves and is practical for the homeowner. Pantry staples always look better when housed in a collection of glass canisters.

A carpenter/homeowner crafted the built-in look in a library with shelves made out of tobacco poles and unsanded barn wood, adding the classic Z design to the doors. The hefty scale of the room's rectangular poplar logs adds age-old architectural interest. Black-and-white buffalo-check wing chairs add comfort for reading.

TIP When searching on eBay for large, heavy items, such as a cabinet, appliance, or sofa, use their zip code search feature for your area. Shopping locally will cut down on shipping charges. The item you find might be a good deal, but the shipping charges could negate your savings.

A new house is given architectural interest and a vintage style with old beams and furniture pieces with history. It's possible to have a house full of old items without clutter or fuss.

Dark hinges and doorknobs punctuate the whitewashed walls and beadboard cabinets. Dark countertops, dining table, and stained heart pine floors add dramatic punch with a nod to the past. Washable chair slipcovers have relaxed appeal.

Mid-Century Modern

Combine furnishings from different eras for high impact. For example, use 1950s-style chairs with a farmhouse table. Something from the past can enhance a modern interior. If the found objects are treated as works of art, they are often elevated far beyond their humble beginnings. Adding a bit of history warms up the environment.

Sometimes all it takes to make a room come alive is a reclaimed door or window or a remnant of an architectural detail like a piece of an old building hung as art. Arranging an interesting collection is probably the easiest way to transform a room—and appealing collectibles are the most fun to hunt for.

Midcentury chairs are trendy and provide a modern contrast to the metal and wood-plank table. The curtains were made from heavy canvas painters' drop cloths, and the lighting pendant is fashioned after a late 1800s surgical light.

Steel chairs and a massive century-old mahogany dining table pickled a paler hue soften this ultramodern setting. The lamps are repurposed chicken feeders, and the wine rack was found at a flea market.

AMPING UP CHARM WITH VINTAGE

❋ Wicker chairs are easy to find and refresh with spray paint. They don't have to be in perfect condition to look great, but the seats must be intact to be useful.
TIP *Wicker in poor shape is difficult to repair, but a little wear and tear can be more interesting than a perfect piece— just not in the seat.*

❋ Worn quilts don't have to be perfect. Fold them on a shelf. It's a beautiful way to display them. If a quilt is in good shape, hang it on a wall.

❋ Old Indian clubs, a form of nineteenth-century weights, have a lovely sculptural shape and are abundantly easy to find. Group them for an interesting display on a shelf.

❋ Old doors or windows might be all you need to create a focal point of interest in a room.

❋ Use vintage fabric to cover throw pillows on a new sofa.

❋ Memorabilia for framing is abundantly varied and easy to find if you're creative and open-minded. Make a gallery of early black-and-white or sepia family photographs in a powder room.

Repurposed on a Budget

A Texas couple built a vacation retreat and then had little money left for furnishings, so they took the creative approach. "Don't fight your limitations," they advise. "A tight budget forces you to find creative solutions to problems, and the results are always interesting. Our home wouldn't be as unique if we were able to buy everything new." The first thing they did to gather inspiration was create a binder of photos and tear sheets of everything they liked. If you're in the same situation, they say, "Retrain your eye. If you're hunting for a coffee table, for example, expand your search to include items that could *become* a coffee table: a trunk, shipping pallet, even a butcher block perched on oversized lampshade frames."

Interesting vintage window screens were snagged at a yard sale for five dollars apiece, and the coffee table was made from worn pine flooring set on wire lampshade frames. The fireplace was created out of inexpensive drywall, a modern take on adobe.

Slate-gray walls create a dramatic background for framed sections of 1960s wallpaper in a dining room furnished with a salvaged school library table surrounded by recovered midcentury Thonet chairs. The chandelier was created from midcentury pendant lamps wired by an electrician to a single ceiling plate.

An oversized painted wood Moroccan table becomes the centerpiece of a traditional living room enhanced by an oil painting from an estate sale and 1940s chair recovered with wool suiting in a color from the table.

Classic Style

Traditional furnishings work well with salvaged finds. Sometimes all you need to lift a room from being too traditional are a few well-placed, cleverly framed art pieces. One homeowner found charming 1960s wallpaper that depicts pastoral scenes in a folksy style reminiscent of Grandma Moses. She framed panels as wall art. First painting the walls slate-gray gave the room a modern feeling, and the panels pop with color.

Mixing and matching traditional upholstered furniture with a found funky object is always a pleasant surprise in a room. But, if that funky item is functional and practical as well as unusual and good-looking, with a colorful past, it's even better. One smashing item will do the trick. For example, a single mother of two grown children moved from her large family home to a small cottage half the size. She got rid of excess possessions, paring down to just the basic necessities, like an upholstered chair and sofa in her small living room. Then she assessed the room and knew it needed something exotic. This came in the form of a found, painted-wood Moroccan table. Its size and beautiful design, along with its authentic origin, gave the room its personality. A marvelously flamboyant oil portrait was a real find at an estate sale. Suiting wool was used to recover a 1940s chair. It's good to keep in mind that traditional furniture with good, classic lines can be transformed with fabric not necessarily meant for upholstery. Other ideas include sailcloth, shirt cotton, a patchwork quilt, and remnants of different vintage fabrics like a linen tablecloth.

Lighting is a terrific way to mix things up in a traditional room. Pay homage to America's past with rugged, industrial-strength verdigris pendants. When placed over a traditional or modern dining table, you'll cast chic in a whole new light.

Industrial chic comes from these eye-catching sheet metal fixtures, an elegant take on standard rugged shop lamps.

Cottage Chic

This style is an informal, mismatched, casual look that seems as though it just happened—like an English garden that has been growing as if unattended, even though it was planned out impeccably and treated lovingly. A comfortable "come on in and grab a seat" attitude can be created with care and lots of tweaking—and then you forget about it and let it evolve over time. It's a knack that's worth cultivating and can be very satisfying, if this is the lifestyle you're after.

One of the great things about a cottage look is that it's easy to achieve and inexpensive to create. It's all about maximizing the things you already have. Before buying things to fill your house, check what you have. You might be surprised at how much you can recycle, perhaps from family hand-me-downs, to get the cottage look you're after. And best of all, cottage style is rather inexpensive in the scheme of things.

To modernize an old cottage, dark wood can be painted white, combining rustic with bright and youthful. It's a clean look and goes so well with punctuations of green, especially living plants. What else goes with this look? Painted floors benefit from rag rugs or perhaps a kilim with a stencil treatment using soft celadon and ivory colors, for example, to create a checkerboard or diamond pattern. Simple pine, weathered, or painted furniture is part of cottage chic. Don't be fooled by the simplicity of this style. It's actually quite sophisticated when done well.

Sheer café curtains are delicate enough to let light in but also provide privacy (think summer breezes blowing through open windows). An alternative would be wooden plantation shutters. Wicker is a material associated with cottage style and so is gently worn or faded small floral-print vintage cotton fabric on cushions and pillows. Mattress ticking is less cottagey, more sophisticated.

Outdoor Dining

There are many options for creating outdoor living spaces where good weather is consistent year-round. Those who live in places where seasons change have to be more weather conscious about the materials they use. One couple created a simple eating area on a back patio overlooking their garden. The furniture is weather resistant and easy to take inside during the winter months. Using a round piece of marble for the top, they fashioned a table using old railroad ties for the legs. Their chairs were made from repurposed oil drums, and a creamware pitcher is a simple accessory filled with hydrangeas from the garden.

Cottage chic includes an array of vintage finds like this painted hutch, pine farm table, and metal bistro chairs. The peeling paint authenticates the chairs. A collection of milk glass dishware fills the hutch. The white on white punctuated with green is a comfortable, fresh scheme.

"An outdoor room should be as comfortable as an indoor one," says a New York homeowner. When the weather warms up, he brings out wicker benches, daybeds, side tables, and Adirondack chairs. Many are junk-store finds. "I like to be sure each area has its own personality," he says. Shopping for things to fill an outdoor garden dining room is fun. Every room should complement its surroundings and vice versa. "We painted a U-Haul's worth of beat-up furniture egg-white and yellow to go with the flowers growing in the garden," he adds. "The outdoor rooms are designed so the décor is the main focus. The plants are just icing on the cake." This is good advice. If you're planning an outdoor eating area, use your garden for inspiration when it comes to style and color. If your garden is formal or you have planters around a deck or patio, you might not want wicker and rusted metal. On the other hand, a more casual garden would suggest mismatched, perhaps weathered furniture. A long table made from salvaged wood with painted bistro chairs might be perfect for family gatherings.

A dining table was made with a round piece of marble and railroad tie legs. The chairs are made from repurposed oil drums.

Mismatched woven chairs and a teak table set the scene for meals in the backyard. Wicker and reed are fairly durable all-weather materials.

A wicker rocker is brought back to life with a coat of hunter-green spray paint. The cushions were recovered with a vibrant vintage throw. Wall art is created with antique game pieces: old tennis rackets and croquet mallets.

Wicker

Adding a delightful romantic feeling to any room, wicker furniture is perfect for a porch. Natural wicker has been popular for centuries, and while it looks delicate, it is actually quite strong. Look for wicker in good condition, especially the seats. It's difficult and often expensive to get wicker repaired. A coat of spray paint can instantly change the look to go with your décor. But wicker is lovely when aged, so leaving it as is can be more desirable. Wicker is easy to clean with soap and water.

Don't overlook old books as wall art. In this living room, Douglas fir shelves display books that were passed down through the homeowner's family.

This outdoor room was built from scratch with everything including a sense of history. Wicker chairs surround the coffee table fashioned out of a reclaimed wine barrel.

A bookcase across one living room wall holds interesting objects that work well as a visual arrangement, much like a painting.

Smart Storage and Displays

A full wall of bookcases in a living room is a good way to add cottage chic when the assortment of items is artistic and creatively planned. For example, you might arrange architectural salvage, flea market figurines, and a midcentury clock. Add to this an assortment of carefully chosen books, a vase of flowers, and small paintings. Consider displaying plates and perhaps painted wooden candlesticks. When everything is white, the shapes and sizes of the items become the art. Books provide the color. Take the opportunity to arrange them in a pleasing way. Edit, add, stand back, and rearrange until you are satisfied. Then do it again. It's a work in progress.

Keep plates and glasses in an open cabinet for easy access in the dining room. To make it look good, you might hunt for an old hutch that you can repurpose with new paint, glass panels, and chicken wire. To hide clutter, staple-gun drop-cloth material inside glass cabinet doors. The material is cheap, and once you wash it, the coarse cotton becomes soft and pliable. Unbleached muslin is an alternative.

Repurposed barn wood and steel pipes conjure a vintage mail-sorting station. The cubby-filled storage units corral items in (highly organized) style.

This cabinet was once two separate pieces assembled one on top of the other. To unify it as one cabinet, paint or stain it all one color. Drop cloth (from a paint or hardware store) creates cover inside glass doors.

Farmhouse Style

American farmhouses embodied the need for basic comfort and were practical and pleasant in design. Sturdy and well crafted, they were built to last. These family homesteads, modest in scale and size, often present the perfect canvas for renovation and restoration due to the original materials used to build them. Typical are large wooden ceiling beams, wood paneling on the walls, and wide pine floorboards. Depending on the condition of the house, some homeowners choose to incorporate saved items with things that need replacing, like appliances, windows, doors, and furnishings. However, others rehab the home by refurbishing with paint, sanding floors, adding stain, and generally creating a farmhouse framework for traditional or modern furniture.

A Connecticut couple embraced all the imperfections and original details of their eighteenth-century farmhouse and used a spare decorating approach to enhance them. Although the paint was peeling and the uneven floorboards creaked, when the owners first saw the farmhouse, they said, "Old beams and loose doorknobs are high on the list of things we look for." These are the things that give a house character. They were committed to keeping the house as they found it, although a new kitchen was a must. However, dramatic architecture—rough-hewn beams and pitched ceilings—call for simplicity in decorating.

To create a farmhouse style in a not-so-old house, look for these elements at salvage yards to incorporate into your home. For example, you might cover one wall with salvaged wood panels left as is or painted white. Worn wood, when sanded and stained, is an easy way to add just a touch of that appealing farmhouse style. Whatever material you use, it should be honest, unpretentious, and homey.

The only thing better than a truly great buy? Dozens upon dozens of them. That's what an owner of a North Carolina bungalow believes. "Rustic accessories like license plates and coffee tins are perfect for vintage displays and storage," she says. "Sometimes, as is the case with chairs, reproductions are sturdier than the originals, so I recovered the cushions in a speckled oilcloth to add pattern and durability." The planked walls in the dining room were made from shipping pallets. A creamy white paint was needed to give the rustic material a fresh finish. As I have said many times, paint is the cheapest, easiest, and best instant gratification starting point for any home project.

For the ultimate farmhouse-style breakfast room, a homeowner mixed a hefty trestle-based table with antique ladder-back and Windsor chairs and a polished nickel chandelier. The soft sea-breeze paint color and reclaimed beams evoke earlier times. Built-in plate racks make accessing plates easy from the kitchen or dining area.

The dining table is made from wide pine boards, stained and waxed to a soft sheen. Walls are made from freshly painted shipping crates, and the hanging light fixture was once a porch light that just needed some cleaning.

Imperfect original details are highlighted when the furnishings are spare. The boat propeller and oil paintings came from a secondhand store.

For a jolt of modernism, the steel bistro chairs are new. A mid-1800s portrait is just right against the dining area's original wood paneling.

CREATING AN EATING AREA IN A SMALL COTTAGE KITCHEN:

1 Hang reclaimed open shelves or glass-fronted cabinets. Give a country favorite a twist with non-matching shelves hung on a single wall. Selected for practicality, they also add a dose of humble charm. Cottage style rejects anything "matchy." Mismatched is always more interesting.

2 Creamy white-painted walls and whitewashed wooden floors (topped with three coats of polyurethane) make a small space seem larger.

3 A bench offers equal seating to a host of chairs but can be tucked under the table when not in use.

4 Find vintage cooking utensils, storage bins, canisters, and wooden bowls and spoons for everyday use. These items add cozy warmth to a white room.

Every square inch in a cottage kitchen is outfitted with salvage-style repurposed materials and accessories to double as a dining area.

After scoring an authentic farmhouse table on Craigslist, a thrifty homeowner with a down-home style collected antique bentwood chairs over time. Wicker chairs (one at each end of the table), buffalo-check curtains, and a weathered hutch round out the come-as-you-are vibe.

A dining room hutch displays vintage glass bottles and vintage dishes, including yellowware, ironstone, and glass and metal pieces. The steel-gray color of the hutch is a dramatic background for the light-colored items. Soft and worn white linen napkins are piled on one shelf.

Another homeowner renovated a farmhouse built in 1745, restoring its wide-plank floors, exposed beams, and original paned glass windows. Then she filled it with a mix of flea market finds and pretty florals, and revitalized it with a fresh décor. When you start with an early home that already exudes authenticity, decorating with modern elements like a clear acrylic coffee table, for example, invigorates the interior. Bright fabrics, fresh paint, lively rugs, and lots of plants in interesting planters go a long way toward highlighting the wonderful vintage elements in the construction. When new meets old, the result is a youthful energy with historic charm.

The sunroom's salvaged casement windows from the butler's pantry of a rundown Victorian house, vintage fireplace surround, and thick old beams provide a wonderful background for modern furnishings. Live plants and pots of flowers make any room cheerful.

Wall Art

A wall of thrift store paintings of the same subject can have even more impact than a single, more expensive piece. And mixing up the theme by throwing in something of total contrast makes it more interesting. For example, a Texas homeowner and lifelong collector created down-home charm on a dime by combining floral art, framed with thrift store and yard sale frames, with a vintage camp sign just for fun.

A weathered painted table that was once a school desk is left just as found. Patina that occurs organically is prettier than the done-in-a-day variety. An unexpected addition to the floral painting arrangement is the vintage camp sign.

A wide chair rail was designed to accommodate artwork—
no nails necessary. Vintage bird prints lean against the wall
and dot the entryway's shelving unit. The worn birdcage
was found in an antique shop. Bird nests, milk glass, and
hotel trays are arranged on each shelf.

An eclectic grouping of wall art includes an assortment of
subject matter that makes the gallery wall sophisticated—
architectural drawings, portraits, and botanical prints.
The finishing touch to this formula is a a three-dimensional
object, like the pair of antlers.

The secret to getting a high-end look for less is splurging in small doses. Pay up for small quantities of expensive fabrics, like the block-printed pillows on a former church pew.

Mountain Retreat

A California resident has had a passion for fixing up houses for as long as he can remember. His first fixer-upper was a dilapidated midcentury cottage, then he relocated to a crumbling bungalow, followed by a 1920s cottage, and then a century-old farmhouse. As an inveterate renovator, he says, "Remodeling has always been my secret sideline." After that, he and his partner headed to Massachusetts to renovate houses full-time, opening a design firm to turn old houses into vacation rentals. One of those houses became their own personal getaway.

"It was dark, dingy, and depressing," he said. But the house had one great feature: a massive stone fireplace that faced outside onto a porch. They enclosed the area to create a den with an open kitchen on the other side of the fireplace. They installed windows to take advantage of the views of nature and covered the walls in pine paneling. Whenever a room is dark, look for ways to install windows, French doors, or whatever it takes to bring in nature.

Rather than tartans and twiggy furniture to go with the environment, they chose molded plastic chairs from the 1960s, a marble-top table, and clean-lined sofas slipcovered in ivory and taupe canvas. **Tip:** Sailcloth and drop cloth fabrics are good slipcover material. Heavy unbleached muslin, washed and softened, is another good material.

The reclaimed porch and outdoor stone fireplace were enclosed to create an open living room and kitchen made from reclaimed wood. Colors are muted and furnishings spare. Accessories include a hand-blown glass vase and a vintage kindling bucket. A repainted tray is set on top of a sturdy pouf for a coffee table.

Casters attached to the bottom of a vintage chicken crate turn it into an interesting coffee table.

On a Budget

Dying for something with personality, a young couple opted for a fixer-upper rather than a new home. "We didn't have the money for the size home we needed, but we know how to repurpose old things and had the confidence to find creative solutions for the things we needed," they said. For example, a vintage chicken crate became a coffee table when two-dollar casters were attached to the bottom. This is a good example of how to marry objects to make them work for you. You don't have to be a super craftsperson or particularly handy to create useful furnishings from salvage. In fact, the materials you find are deliberately rough and crudely made, since most were put to good practical use without a thought toward aesthetics. It's how we view this material today, and how we employ it, that elevates it to good design.

A good example of this is the wall art. They found a distressed piece of wood and painted the number 5 on it for the number of people in their family. Sanding gave it an aged finish. Globes collected from thrift stores and tag sales top a set of three filing cabinets from Goodwill spray-painted yellow and topped with stained plywood. "New stuff doesn't usually have the character we love—the rust, the chipped paint, the history," they explain. And what they created did not take craftsmanship, but it did take a creative eye to come up with a good design idea for using cast-off materials. Seeing how someone else did it can be inspiring.

Textiles

Homespun blankets, an early American quilt, and a lace tablecloth have the potential to become visual headboards. One homeowner says, "My favorite textiles have the maker's name or the date stitched into the corners."

Three secondhand filing cabinets spray-painted and topped with wood create a storage unit.

An 1854 homespun blanket serves as a headboard. The wall art is pressed sea kelp found at a Paris flea market.

Grain sack upholstery enlivens the armchairs in this living room, and the homeowner turned kerosene canisters into lamps. A wicker table was given new life with spray paint and topped with glass.

Two reclaimed living room chairs are clad in two antique fabrics, and a wash bucket was covered with glass for a coffee table. The vintage wire basket holds wood or magazines, depending on the season.

Little Things with Big Impact

"I never buy anything that will only look good in one spot," a homeowner says. "If I find something I like, I buy it and know in my heart of hearts that I will find a place for it no matter if I have to get rid of something to make room." This homeowner likes accessories that are oversized, like the weathered clock face that once hung on Paris's Boulevard Saint-Germain in the late 1800s. "I just happened upon it at a flea market and could not resist," she says. "I knew it was too big in scale for most of my rooms, but when I got it home and hung it on a shiplap wall in the living room, it was dynamite. It just made the room." The wall treatment, stained a cloudy gray, also includes a pine-clad ceiling. Decorating with something dramatic, even oversized, can make a room.

A weathered clock's face is a dramatic accessory on a painted pine-covered wall. It came from a French flea market.

Oversized and dramatic, a salvaged train station clock hangs above a tableau of taxidermied birds. Secondhand chairs were reupholstered in nubby linen.

Small Areas

Make the most of a narrow wall space. For example, one homeowner turned a narrow wall at the end of a dining room into a bar area. First she chose an off-black paint color for this wall alone. A wonderfully worn and warped table stands out against this color as if it were a piece of sculpture. Underneath she created a display that includes a wicker locker for glasses and an old-fashioned suitcase for linens. You might have a similar space, but that doesn't mean you have to have these items. What you find will be totally unique, and you'll create a vignette with items that respond to your needs.

A light fixture from an Ohio barn creates an unusual piece of architecture over a reclaimed table in a breakfast nook.

A bar area was created on top of a worn table and vintage wicker trunk. The hand-painted lamp is one of a pair scored at a local thrift shop.

Picks from Barns and Factories

"Old barns have the best picks, but old factories are also cool," says an inveterate picker who follows dirt roads through sleepy towns in search of gems from bygone eras. "But once you get them home," he says, "the trick is figuring out how to use them." He goes on to say, "I got my start as a picker by combing through farms for old bicycles, then moved on to other items." Some of the coolest items he says he found are wire lockers from a factory that he uses as storage in a hallway, a light fixture from an Ohio barn that he hung over a dining table, old cowboy boots "just for display," and a weathervane in the dining room that came out of an attic in a sixth-generation-owned house. It blew off the barn in 1938. Everything tells a story.

Barn doors, poplar panels, and ropes are all ripe for repurposing in a new home. When a couple built a barn-like home, they let it evolve over time, rather than rushing through the process. The result was a long, barn-inspired structure with one large open living area. Though barns are traditionally without windows, this homeowner's interpretation features large windows (some are 10 feet tall) to integrate the views into the design.

A small workspace was created with a small antique table that fits perfectly between two windows. An antique bedspring is a show-stopping memo board, and a sweet metal chair was covered with a piece of stenciled burlap. The curtain rods are made from piping.

Lockers from a factory are used to store gear in a narrow hallway area.

"My goal when building the house," says the homeowner, "was to choose materials that could take a beating and were in keeping with the barn aesthetic. Nothing too delicate." Among those selections: white oak plank floors secured with vintage square-head nails, a limestone mantel, and a fieldstone fireplace. Poplar paneling in varying widths and hung vertically was painted creamy white. It accentuates the soaring 15-foot ceilings. Sliding barn doors with a traditional Z-brace frame are striking in the upstairs hallway. "Light fixtures are a key part of the design," he adds.

Barn wood was used everywhere when building this expansive home: for doors, walls, window shutters, and some of the furniture.

GROCERY

Sliding barn doors not only add country appeal, but also they're great space savers.

VINTAGE AMERICA FLAGS

In 1912, President Taft issued an executive order setting out guidelines for the country's flag. Prior to that, makers were free to interpret the configuration of white stars in a blue field as they saw fit. Some stitched them in straight rows (as we do today); others created a concentric circle or a single large star made up of smaller ones. The resulting variety of designs makes flags predating the ordinance prized collectibles.

CHAPTER 3

Bedrooms

A spindle four-poster Jenny Lind–style bed is covered with an antique quilted coverlet.
The walls are covered with salvaged flooring. The owner wisely kept its original worn turquoise paint.

Start with a Good Bed!

Never use a secondhand mattress! This is an absolute rule. If you spend money on one thing, it must always be the mattress. After that, you can look for an interesting headboard. By committing to a mattress, you'll know the exact size headboard or frame you need and won't be tempted by the fabulous double headboard you uncover, when you know you want a queen-sized bed. Early beds were usually smaller than what is made today, so even a twin frame might not fit a twin mattress by today's standards.

My daughter bought two early mahogany spindle bed frames at an auction, only to find it impossible to get mattresses to fit. In the end, she had to have them custom-made, totally negating the great buy she got on the frames.

An Arkansas homeowner says, "My husband and I tend to fall in love with dilapidated houses. I love walls with a great weathered look." If a room doesn't have it, she knows how to create the look she loves.

Salvaged boards cover the walls of this master bedroom, and a delicate 1920s eyelet coverlet softens the room. A length of Victorian porch trim provides free-standing artwork.

A mix of finishes proves black and brown go together. Brass sconces cast warm reading light, and a vintage chandelier hangs from the salvaged and repainted ceiling boards. A vintage quilt and pillow covers are timeless.

Another creative homeowner in Nashville, Tennessee, says she's a born picker and loves decorating the homes of friends and family members just for the fun of it. Using a mix of carefully chosen pieces, neutral colors, and treasured family keepsakes, she transformed her Nashville home into a tireless space. "I never buy pieces that will only work on one particular wall or in one particular room in the house," she says. "I look for things that will hold up over time." When she can't find the original of a piece of furniture she wants, this savvy lady opts for a reproduction. For example, she wanted an antique wrought-iron canopy bed like the one that belonged to her grandmother and found a new one that she says is a close match. It's the style she was after, and that's what she got. She found a simple pine dresser that toughens up the feminine look of the room. She says, "The older I get, the more I want to focus on items that will tell our story. I want to fill my house not only with inherited things from my family, but items worthy of passing down to my children."

A pretty vintage linen tablecloth is used as a coverlet.

Vintage Linens

These fabrics are not just for the bed. They make nice curtains or slipcovers, as well. When used on pillows, they introduce color and texture to a white room. In eighteenth-century England, a tea towel was a special drying cloth used to dry precious and expensive china tea things. Retro fabrics with prints like cherries and baskets of flowers can be found at flea markets. However, they are also being reproduced and can be used to make your own vintage accessories. In fact, you can instantly age new fabric by soaking it in a tea bath. To make it soft and worn-looking, wash it with a small amount of bleach and then rinse with fabric softener.

A quilted cotton bedcover, duvet cover made from old mattress ticking, and pillow covers from vintage fabric dress a painted pine bed. A little side table is left as is, with original peeling paint.

FABRIC FOR VINTAGE ACCESSORIES

❁ Cover pillows with remnants of upholstery fabric for an elegant, rich look.

❁ For country charm, use calico prints.

❁ Homespun fabric is associated with early American households.

❁ Use soft printed-cotton sheeting for a cottage chic look.

❁ An old chenille bedspread can be cut up for pillow covers.

❁ Even a worn quilt can be cut apart for curtains or pillow covers, or folded on a shelf.

❁ Burlap and grain sacks can be repurposed as a curtain to hide pots and pans under a sink where there is no cabinet.

❁ Red or blue and white gingham is pure farmhouse country style.

A headboard is slipcovered in vintage linens. Square mirror frames are made from barn wood.

The headboard was made from tin panels, the steamer trunk holds extra blankets, and the antique barn door saves space as a bathroom door. The track was found at a tractor-supply store.

Style on a Budget

A couple with an eye for salvage but on a tight budget designed two bedrooms in their home for very little money and a whole lot of ingenuity. "Being on a budget forced us to find things we could repurpose," they say, "and that was part of the fun." After spending money on good mattresses, they had little left for everything else. However, for twenty-five dollars, they found a door and pallets at a flea market and used them to create the headboard and base of a daybed in a guest room. Next, for ten dollars apiece, they turned cow-feed sifters into artful sconces with burlap fringe. For a little over two dollars a square foot, they picked up an odd assortment of wood planks at a Habitat for Humanity ReStore and used it to cover the ceiling. Feed grain sacks worked for throw pillow covers, and the whole room came together with unusual style. The addition of two pouf ottomans and an inexpensive cotton rug completed the look they envisioned. An odd little side table was easy to clean up. Nightstands don't have to match, and it's relatively easy to come across unusual tables for this purpose. Longleaf pine shelving from a dismantled lumberyard now covers the floor. "We like things that are torn, tattered, and yellowed. Practically everything here is on its second or third life."

For the master bedroom, they used tin panels, twenty dollars apiece, to simulate a headboard, and a steamer trunk found at a garage sale for twenty-five dollars holds extra blankets. To save on space, an antique barn door is suspended from a track found for one hundred dollars at a tractor-supply store. The door cost less than two hundred dollars. The homeowner cut a small window in the door to allow natural light into the bathroom.

A bed swathed in vintage linens gives texture to the all-white bedroom. Sliding barn doors free up floor space in a small bedroom. The walls are covered in pine planks that have been pickled.

A guest room on a budget includes a repurposed door for the headboard and pallets used to make a base for the daybed. Cow-feed sifters provide creative lighting for a song.

It's All in the Details

Little things go a long way toward making a big impact. Antique doorknobs, hinges, and tassels attached to silk ropes for drapery tiebacks all add an opulent look to a bedroom. These can often be found in antique shops and online auctions. **Warning:** Before buying doorknobs, be sure all parts are intact and will fit the door you have in mind. I once bought oval porcelain doorknobs at a secondhand stall in Florence, Italy, only to find they had to be retrofitted at great expense when I got home. Glass doorknobs are attractive on bedroom and closet doors and are easy to find. A good source is House of Antique Hardware (www.houseofantiquehardware.com).

When talking about a guest bedroom in her home, she says, "If I had put up chintz wallpaper, you wouldn't notice anything else. A neutral palette reveals the nuances of old things." She found a late 1800s French dress form and a small antique side table just right for holding a retro-designed alarm clock. Sometimes you'll find items that simply appeal to you but may not necessarily be useful. The dress form is a good example of this. But the homeowner loved it and found a way to use it as a decorative object that gives the room a bit of joie de vivre.

A neutral palette reveals the nuances of old things.

An antique rope bed was retrofitted with metal supports to hold modern box springs. Old beams were added to give an attic bedroom farmhouse charm.

METAL NAME PLATES affixed to fiberboard shelves gives them a vintage look and make sorting a cinch.

Clever idea: The owner used a ripped leopard-print coat to upholster a whimsical chair to accompany a 1920s ebony desk. An African feather headdress and a black-and-white photo of Paris make for an eclectic mix.

Furniture with Purpose

When looking for ways to gain storage, think creatively. For example, an old orchard ladder just leaning against a bedroom wall is perfect for holding extra blankets in a bedroom.

Old bureaus are easy to come by, and if they're not in perfect condition, they can be sanded and stained or painted if the wood isn't exceptional. Changing the pulls or knobs can make a big difference.

A rough-hewn item was once an orchard ladder. Now it holds extra blankets. The found lamp base just needed a new lampshade to modernize it, and the wall art from the 1950s came from a paint-by-numbers kit. (A quick Etsy search yielded seven thousand results.)

Reproductions of nineteenth-century prints (a whaling scene and a diagram of weather vanes) hang above the bedroom's pine dresser that was unearthed at a Connecticut antique shop. Porcelain knob replacements give it a modern flair.

To make a bedroom with high ceilings feel cozy, the homeowner rose to the challenge with a tester bed (the columns help fill the vertical space), checked curtains to create a cocoon-like effect, and dressers rather than night tables. The kilim rug and distressed furniture reinforce the "collected over time" aesthetic.

Eke out space at the end of a bedroom for a home office. A spindle leg table can easily be found in dark mahogany. The super-shiny blue lacquer finish catapults this piece to the cutting edge. The gilt-edged armchair is an elegant addition.

Vintage Wallpaper

Popular in New England in the early 1700s, wallpaper was sold by stationers, booksellers, and specific merchants who specialized in "imported luxury goods." At the time it was expensive but affordable when compared to other decorative techniques, such as hand-painting.

By the mid-eighteenth century, floral patterns were popular and went with the brocades and chintzes of the time. The website Historic New England (historicnewengland.org) brings wallpaper into the twentieth century and is searchable by date, location, manufacturer, and keywords like color and type of pattern.

A couple in Oregon designed and built a house on a tight budget and say, "Even if we had all the money in the world, we'd still hunt down bargains and repurpose things to make our home quirky and charming." Vintage-looking wallpaper with a large-scale motif eliminates the need for art and can set the tone in a bedroom. Pillows made from old grain sacks can be paired with new bedding, and there's always the opportunity to add style with unusual night tables. Look for a dresser and perhaps a chair to round out the charming, old-fashioned, romantic look that began with the wallpaper.

Large tree trunks, cut at different heights, were used as nightstands in a master bedroom.

Child's Room with a Theme

When planning her young son's bedroom, a California mom used a circus theme. "I found a framed poster advertising a 1930s circus, and that became the focus of the room," she said. She purchased the cherry bed at a local antiques mall and added new stuffed animals. A wicker trunk holds extra bed linens.

A framed circus poster from the 1930s becomes the focal point of a child's room.

Small Spaces

Look for unused spaces like nooks and crannies under eaves or stairways, above doorways and kitchen cabinets to reclaim and repurpose for your needs. For example, when a homeowner cleaned out a storage space with a cedar ceiling, she was able to create a quiet writing nook. All it took was a small antique table and chairs and a lovely hand-painted lamp. The floors were reclaimed and brightened up with a white pickling technique. Even a closet can be turned into an office with salvaged wood for custom-made shelves and a desktop. All the accessories might come from yard sales or antique shops. When you design a small area such as this, it becomes a creative challenge that is totally doable. Consider a barn door on a track to close up your office at the end of the day.

Salvaged wood was used to create a board-and-batten storage shed.

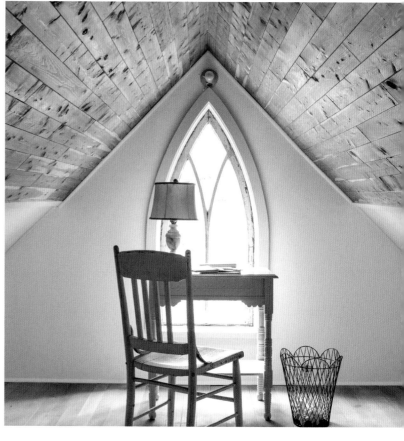

A writing nook was carved out of a small attic storage space. Pine floors are pickled white, but the cedar ceiling was left as is.

An Unusual Guest Cottage

"I love putting puzzles together," says one homeowner. "I take all the salvaged pieces other people have given me and make something unusual." The result: a chicken coop transformed into a guest cottage. He used all reclaimed wood to create a charmingly rustic bedroom, adding 1940s poplar headboards painted with delightful floral details and turning an old metal washtub into a nightstand.

A chicken coop is turned into a guest cottage with weathered salvaged wood on the interior.

Closets

A homeowner who considers herself a master problem solver said, "If I wasn't confident about my 'handyman' abilities, I never would have bought an old house, but it's proven to be a never-ending joy." When she found that her recently purchased early house was shy on closet space, she set out to find a solution. "I didn't have room in my bedroom to build a closet," she says, "because the roofline is slanted and I wanted to preserve the old ceiling beams. This room was originally an attic." When she found a pair of eight-paned windows in a salvage yard, she grabbed them, "because they cost practically nothing," she said. A stack of barn wood was the next score. As a creative do-it-yourselfer, she knew she could repurpose these raw materials into an armoire, which she did, making it the exact size for the space. With some vintage lace to cover the windows, she had the perfect freestanding closet that fit with the style of the room. From time to time, she displays folded quilts on top of the armoire.

An armoire made from reclaimed paint-worn glass doors, barn wood, and vintage lace.

*A home office was created
in an upstairs landing
area under a sloped roof.*

If you need to eke out space for a home office, heed a tip from one homeowner who took advantage of every square foot of her home. With an upstairs landing under the eaves, she created a full-fledged home office. A desk can be made to the exact size needed with salvaged lumber, or look for an old farmhouse-style kitchen table. Wire chairs have a lighter look than heavy office chairs, and a gooseneck task lamp that either sits on a small base or clamps onto the desktop takes up less space than a traditional lamp.

CHAPTER 4

Bathrooms

In a guest bathroom, sconces flank a 1910 medicine cabinet fitted with a new mirror. With the help of a marble top and Kraus sink set, a weathered table becomes a washstand. A vintage commercial basket holds towels.

A bathroom is perfect for adding a few retro items to make it distinctive. You don't need much, as the room is small. Consider using salvaged materials to cover walls and floors. Retro fixtures also add unexpected character.

An interesting material from the past is pressed tin. It is a lovely way to cover a ceiling or walls. You can leave it as is, or paint it for a period alternative to traditional tiles or beadboard. Many homeowners find that an ornate chandelier adds unexpected elegance to a bathroom.

Complete the bathroom with a retro shower curtain made from vintage fabric. Consider making this item from a quilt, chenille bedspread, or tablecloth, then adding a liner. Circular shower rods are available from renovation supply houses if the curtain is to go around a claw-foot tub.

With the addition of custom-cut mirrors, a cast-off window frame becomes an impressive full-length mirror. A reclaimed door with porcelain doorknob is another salvage find.

Tile is another material for interesting patterns on the floor. A California homeowner converted a small bedroom into a large bathroom and combined a new tub with a vintage look, then added an antique table and milking stool. She covered the floor in terracotta tiles. But the pièce de résistance is an oversized mirror made from a cast-off window frame that fills one wall and an unexpected lighting fixture: an antique chandelier. A bathroom is the perfect place for a full-length mirror. Hardware stores will cut mirrors to fit and size, and a salvaged door or window makes the perfect frame. Another option is to make the frame from barn wood to a size that will fit your space. This is an easy do-it-yourself project and might just be exactly what makes your bathroom exceptional.

All sorts of vintage furniture pieces, from a small cabinet to an armoire, are perfect for storing towels and bathroom accessories. Pedestal sinks, mirrors, vanities, and faucets will add vintage appeal. Found shutters for the windows might do the trick, and if there's room, a weathered chair or a wooden milking stool will provide an interesting addition.

Milking Stools

While many stools for milking cows were factory produced, the most interesting ones are one of a kind, made by farmers from whatever they had on hand. A collector and self-described "milking stool expert" advises: "When buying stools from antique shops, you can tell if it's really a milking stool when you can see where the farmer grabbed it with his dirty hands, and if you just dampen the legs a little and see if they smell of manure."

A reclaimed industrial-style sink, with new brass faucets that only look old, makes a stylish wash station. Cubby-filled storage units corral items in high style.

An old hand-painted metal sign hangs above a salvaged cast-iron tub. A worn painted piano stool is wonderful as is.

CLAW-FOOT TUBS

The most sought-after salvaged items for creating a vintage-looking bathroom, classic claw-foot tubs, whether new or old, are available in sizes from 4 to 6 feet long. Comfortable for bathing due to their graceful shape and depth, they represent a bygone era. Cast-iron reproduction tubs look authentically old, if you can't find or afford an original. They are almost always white, but the exterior can be painted. Since the plumbing typically comes up through the floor, consult a professional plumber about retrofitting your bathroom and be sure your flooring can handle the weight. New reproduction tubs cost in the thousands. So finding one you can restore with paint might be worth the search.

A salvaged claw-foot tub and a 1913 dress form are used to create a unique bathroom. Framed black-and-white photos and drawings fill the wall in a seemingly unplanned and informal layout, appropriate for the look.

With its carved feet and white knobs, the towering gray cabinetry brings all the charm of an antique step-back cupboard with the sturdiness of a modern built-in. On each side, curvy ceramic sinks, simple framed mirrors, and bronze sconces reminiscent of old oil lamps finish the look.

Accessories

Bathroom accessories might include a shelf made from salvaged wood holding a collection of early chinaware for toothbrushes and cosmetics, a white pitcher with a fresh bouquet of wildflowers, a plant, Mason jars to hold cotton balls, and so on. Look for a small wall cabinet to use as a medicine chest, an antique mirror, and old frames for creating an art gallery on the walls. Found memorabilia and old black-and-white photographs offer creative opportunities for wall art. Face the sink cabinet with doors made of old wood and early hardware. And don't overlook vintage faucets for super appeal.

If you can't find old-fashioned faucets like these, Nottingham Brass is a source for reproductions. Despite the sign on the farmhouse sink, the owner claims there's usually plenty of hot water.

A master bathroom sink console incorporates concrete and salvaged wood doors.

Tucked under an antique table, a vintage chest of drawers is used to store towels and bath supplies.

A reclaimed pine mirror hangs over a pedestal sink in a small bathroom. Wire cubbies offer more storage than a medicine chest. The trash can is an old planter.

Short on Space

With only 700 square feet of living space, an apartment dweller had to make every piece count. Inspired by the farmhouse she grew up in, she says, "I like things that are imperfectly beautiful, styled without feeling styled." She refinished creaky floors, and patched cracked walls and washed them with a single coat of high-gloss white. She says that when she gets a creative idea, she doesn't like to overthink it. "I appreciate simplicity." This is good advice. Learn to trust your instincts, and when you think something will work, don't be afraid to go for it.

Even the tiniest powder room can benefit from a well-appointed vintage approach. Look for items that can be repurposed. When you go hunting for unusual objects, for example, look at everything with a creative eye. Ask yourself if something might serve a useful purpose, or if it can be used for something other than the obvious. For example, one homeowner found an old tin planter and used it as a wastebasket. Another turned a wash bucket into a hanging lamp. All sorts of salvaged material can be made into frames for newly cut mirrors, and locker-room gym baskets are perfect for storing towels and other bathroom necessities. Small items, like a collection of milk glass pitchers, can be lined up on a shelf to hold cosmetics and toothbrushes. Don't forget to keep one filled with wildflowers.

A commercial-style sink is fashioned from enameled cast iron, and the zinc-wrapped wooden mirror in a powder room was salvaged from an old house.

SALVAGE SOURCES THROUGHOUT THE COUNTRY

MULTI-STATE EVENT

127 Corridor Sale:
"The World's Longest Yard Sale"
Take Rte. 127 from Alabama to
Michigan, passing near Huntsville,
Alabama; Chattanooga,
Tennessee; Lexington, Kentucky;
Cincinnati, Ohio; Fort Wayne,
Indiana; and Ann Arbor, Michigan
127sale.com

ALABAMA

Southern Accents
308 Second Ave. SE
Cullman, AL 35055
antiques-architectural.com

The Vintage Station
#2 18th Street North
Bessemer, AL 35020
thevintagestation.com

ARIZONA

Architectural Salvage by Ri-Jo
2309 Highway 71 South
Mena, AZ 71953
kingsalvager.net

The Salvage Co.
210 W. Main St.
Superior, AZ 85173
thesalvageco.com

ARKANSAS

2 Brothers Upcycle Store
296 Woodland St.
Menifee, AR (just off I-40, exit 17)
shop2brothers.com

CALIFORNIA

Amighini Architectural
1505 N. State College Blvd.
Anaheim, CA 92806
amighini.net

Olde Good Things
1800 South Grand Ave.
Los Angeles, CA 90015
ogtstore.com

Pasadena Architectural Salvage
2600 E. Foothill Blvd.
Pasadena, CA 91107
pasadenaarchitecturalsalvage.com

Ohmega Salvage
2407 San Pueblo Ave.
Berkeley, CA 94702
ohmegasalvage.com

**Architectural Salvage
of San Diego**
2401 Kettner Blvd.
San Diego, CA 92101
architecturalsalvagesd.com

Alameda Point Antiques Faire
The largest antiques show in
Northern California. Held on
the first Sunday of every month.
The Faire boasts over
800 dealer booths.
alamedapointantiquesfaire.com

COLORADO

Salvage Lady
6400 E. Stapleton Drive S.
Unit A
Denver, CO 80216
salvagelady.com

CONNECTICUT

United Housewrecking
535 Hope St.
Stamford, CT 06906
unitedhousewrecking.com

Irreplaceable Artifacts
428 Main St.
Middletown, CT 06457
irreplaceableartifacts.com

Old Wood Workshop
193 Pomfret Rd.
Pomfret Center, CT 06259
oldwoodworkshop.com

DISTRICT OF COLUMBIA

The Brass Knob
2311 18th St. NW
Washington, DC 20009
thebrassknob.com

FLORIDA

Tampa Bay Salvage
4825 US-19 Alternate
Palm Harbor, FL 34683
tampabaysalvage.com

Circus City Architectural Salvage
1001 Central Ave.
Sarasota, FL 34236
circuscitysalvage.com

Eco Relics
106 Stockton St.
Jacksonville, FL 32204
ecorelics.com

GEORGIA

Metropolitan Artifacts
4783 Peachtree Rd.
Atlanta, GA 30341
metropolitanartifacts.com

Pinch of the Past
2603 Whitaker St.
Savannah, GA 31401
(locations also in Greensboro
and Madison)
pinchofthepast.com

ILLINOIS

A Rustic Garden
854 975 N Ave.
Mt. Sterling, IL 62353
arusticgarden.com

Urban Remains
1850 W. Grand Ave.
Chicago, IL 60622
urbanremainschicago.com

Architectural Artifacts
4325 N. Ravenswood
Chicago, IL 60613
architecturalartifacts.com

Salvage One
1840 W. Hubbard St.
Chicago, IL 60622
salvageone.com

Rebuilding Exchange
1740 W. Webster Ave.
Chicago, IL 60614
rebuildingexchange.org

INDIANA

Doc's Architectural Salvage
1325 W. 30th St.
Indianapolis, IN 46208
docsarchitecturalsalvage.com

**Architectural Antiques
of Indianapolis**
5000 W. 96th St.
Indianapolis, IN 46268
antiquearchitectural.com

White River Salvage
104 West Main St.
Centerville, IN 47330
americanantiquities.com/
whiteriversalvage.html

IOWA

ND MillWerk Salvage and Sales
5617 460th St.
Paulina, IA 51046
oldwoodwork.com

Gavin Historical Bricks
2050 Glendale Rd.
Iowa City, IA 52245
historicalbricks.com

West End Architectural Salvage
22 9th St.
Des Moines, IA 50309
westendsalvage.com

KANSAS

Old Town Architectural Salvage
126 N. Saint Francis St.
Wichita, KS 67202
oldtownarchitecturalsalvage.com

KENTUCKY

Architectural Salvage
614-618 East Broadway
Louisville, KY 40202
architecturalsalvage.com

Cowgirl's Attic
1535 Delaware Ave.
Lexington, KY 40505
cowgirlattic.com

LOUISIANA

The Bank Architectural Antiques
1824 Felicity St.
New Orleans, LA 70119
thebankantiques.com

Ricca's Demolishing Corp.
511 N. Solomon St.
New Orleans, LA 70119
riccasarchitectural.com

MAINE

Portland Architectural Salvage
131 Preble St.
Portland, ME 04101
portlandsalvage.com

Architectural Antiquities
52 Indian Point Lane
Harborside, ME 04642
archantiquities.com

MARYLAND

Second Chance
1700 Ridgely St.
Baltimore, MD 21230
secondchanceinc.org

MASSACHUSETTS

Brimfield Flea Markets
America's oldest outdoor
antiques market
Held three times a year:
May, July, and September
Exhibitors number in
the thousands
277 Main St. (Rte. 131)
Sturbridge, MA 01566
brimfieldantiquefleamarket.com

Restoration Resources
1946 Washington St.
Boston, MA 02118
restorationresources.com

MICHIGAN

Materials Unlimited
2 W. Michigan Ave.
Ypsilanti, MI 48197
materialsunlimited.com

The Heritage Company
150 N. Edwards St.
Kalamazoo, MI 49007
heritagearchitecturalantiques.com

MINNESOTA

Architectural Antiques
1330 Quincy St. NE
Minneapolis, MN 55413
archantiques.com

**North Shore
Architectural Antiques**
224 7th St.
Two Harbors, MN 55616
north-shore-architectural-
antiques.com

City Salvage
2800 Washington Ave. North
Minneapolis, MN 55411
citysalvage.com

MISSISSIPPI

**The Storied Salvage Company
of Jackson MS**
storiedsalvage.com

Old House Depot
639 Monroe St.
Jackson, MS 39202
oldhousedepot.com

MISSOURI

A&O Architectural Salvage
2045 Broadway
Kansas City, MO 64108
aoarchitecturalsalvage.com

Seldom Found
1107 Hickory St.
Kansas City MO 64101
seldomfound.com

Jesse James Antique Mall
12789 County Place Dr.
St. Joseph, MO 64505
jessejamesantiquemall.com

NEVADA

Bloom Vintage Salvage
503 Hotel Plaza
Boulder City, NV 89005
(locations also in Las Vegas
and Henderson)
bloombc.com

NEW HAMPSHIRE

Nor'East Architectural Antiques
16 Exeter Road (Rte. 150)
South Hampton, NH 03827
noreast1.com

Architectural Salvage, Inc.
3 Mill St.
Exeter, NH 03833
oldhousesalvage.com

NEW JERSEY

Olde Good Things
2 Somerset St.
Hopewell, NJ 08525
ogtstore.com

Recycling the Past
381 N. Main St.
Barnegat, NJ 08005
recyclingthepast.com

Amighini Architectural
246 Beacon Ave.
Jersey City, NJ 07306
amighini.net

NEW MEXICO

La Puerta Originals
4523 State Road, Highway 14
Santa Fe, NM 87508
lapuertaoriginals.com

NEW YORK

Historic Houseparts
528-540 South Ave.
Rochester, NY 14620
historichouseparts.com

Silver Fox Salvage
20 Learned St.
Albany, NY 12207
silverfoxsalvage.com

ReHouse
469 W. Ridge Road
Rochester, NY 14615
rehouse.com

Zaborski Emporium
27 Hoffman St.
Kingston, NY 12401
stanthejunkman.com

Olde Good Things
149 Madison Ave.
New York, NY 10016

302 Bowery
New York, NY 10012

5 East 16th St.
New York, NY 10003
ogtstore.com

The Demolition Depot
and Irreplaceable Artifacts
216 E. 125 St.
New York, NY 10035
irreplaceableartifacts.com

Hoffman's Barn
19 Old Farm Road
Red Hook, NY 12571
hoffmansbarn.com

NORTH CAROLINA

Preservation Greensboro
447 W. Washington St.
PO Box 13136
Greensboro, NC 27415
preservationgreensboro.org

OHIO

Columbus Architectural Salvage
1580 Clara St.
Columbus, OH 43211
columbusarchitecturalsalvage.
com

Toledo Architectural Artifacts
20 S. Ontario St.
Toledo, OH 43604
coolstuffiscoolstuff.com

OKLAHOMA

Oklahoma Barn Market
oklahomabarnmarket.com

OREGON

Aurora Mills
14971 First St. NE
Aurora, OR 97002

70 SE Salmon St.
Portland, OR 97214
auroramills.com

Old Portland Hardware
& Architectural
700 NE 22nd Ave.
Portland, OR 97232
oldportlandhardware.com

PENNSYLVANIA

Philadelphia Salvage Company
2234 W. Westmoreland St.
Philadelphia, PA 19140
philadelphiasalvage.com

Construction Junction
214 N. Lexington St.
Pittsburgh, PA 15208
constructionjunction.org

Olde Good Things
400 Gilligan St.
Scranton, PA 18508
ogstore.com

RHODE ISLAND

Aardvark Antiques
9 JT Connell Highway
Newport, RI 02840
aardvarkantiques.com

SOUTH CAROLINA

Old House Salvage
95 Big Survey Rd.
Piedmont, SC 29673
theoldhousesalvage.com

TENNESSEE

Doc's Architectural Salvage
200 E. 9th Ave.
Springfield, TN 37172
docsarchitecturalsalvage.com

Preservation Station
1809 8th Ave.
Nashville, TN 37203
thepreservationstation.com

TEXAS

Memorial Antiques and Interiors
8719 and 8731 Katy Freeway
Houston, TX 77024
ogtstore.com

Old Is Better Than New
1505 Fredericksburg Road
San Antonio, TX 78201
old-sa.com

Country Accents Antiques
8312 Highway 16
(between Bandera and Pipe Creek)
TX
countryaccentsantiques.com

RainBird Rustic Furniture, Art,
and Antique Gallery
103 Main St.
Blanco, TX 78606
rainbirdgalleryonline.com

Burnet Antique Mall
206 S. Main St.
Burnet, TX 78611
burnetantiquemall.com

Round Top Antiques Fair
Giant Antique Fairs twice a year
Big Red Barn Event Center 5 miles
north of the Round Top Square
475 Texas Highway 237 So.
Carmine, TX 78932
roundtoptexasantiques.com

Finds! Of All Kinds
901 U.S. 1
Burnet, TX 78611
findsofallkinds.net

Carol Hicks Bolton Antiquities
301 S. Lincoln St.
Fredericksburg, TX
carolhicksbolton.com

Lone Star Antique Mall
905 East Main St.
Fredericksburg, TX 78624
lonestarmallfbg.com

Adkins Architectural Antiques
and Treasures
3515 Fannin St.
Houston, TX 77004
adkinsantiques.com

VERMONT

Architectural Salvage Warehouse
11 Maple Street, Five Corners
Essex Junction, VT 05452
greatsalvage.com

VIRGINIA

Black Dog Salvage
902 13th St. SW
Roanoke, VA 24016
blackdogsalvage.com

Caravati's Architectural Salvage
104 E. 2nd Ave.
Richmond, VA 23224
caravatis.com

WASHINGTON

Earthwise Architectural Salvage
3447 4th Ave. S
Seattle, WA 98134

628 E. 60th St.
Tacoma, WA 98404
ewsalvage.com

Seattle Building Salvage
seattlebuildingsalvage.com

WISCONSIN

Crescent Moon Antiques
and Salvage
537 N. Main St.
Oshkosh, WI 54901
crescentmoonantiquesandsalvage.com

I.M. Salvage
737 W. Cleveland Ave.
Milwaukee, WI 53215
imsalvage.net

ABOUT THE AUTHOR

Leslie Linsley is the author of over seventy books on crafts, lifestyle, and decorating, including *Nantucket Island Living, Key West: A Tropical Lifestyle,* and *Country Living Aged To Perfection.* Leslie writes a weekly column and blog, *At Home With Leslie Linsley,* for the *Nantucket Inquirer & Mirror* and *Key West Citizen.* Her work is featured in national magazines as well as monthly in *Nantucket Today,* She has been a guest on *Good Morning America, The Today Show,* and *Oprah.* Leslie lives on Nantucket Island with her graphic designer husband and partner Jon Aron. Leslie Linsley's branded product line of home furnishings is sold through upscale home furnishings stores.

Website: leslielinsley.com
Blog: At Home With Leslie Linsley, http://leslielinsley.com/blog-2/

IMAGE CREDITS

Cover photography © Vibeke Svenningsen: front; © Christopher Baker: back top right; © Max Kim-Bee: back bottom left; © Aimee Herring: back top left; © Mark Lohman: back bottom right

© Jean Allsopp: 36, 73, 82; © Christopher Baker: 4, 92, 93 left, 97, 126, 141, 151 top; © Stacey Brandford: 12; © Monica Buck: 38–39, 109, 137 right; © Paul Costello: 11, 31, 116, 121, 123 left, 127; © Zach Desart: 101; © Trevor Dixon: 91; © Sarah Dorio: 30, 32; © Miki Duisterhof: 72, 106, 142; Alison Gootee: 59 left, 98, 125 right; © John Gruen: 61, 74, 83, 111, 132; © Alec Hemer: 1, 3, 33, 56, 66 top, 71, 75, 84, 108, 117, 134 left, 139, 146; © Aimee Herring: 85, 99, 105 right, 143, 152; © Max Kim-Bee: 14, 23, 26, 34, 37, 43, 45, 53 right, 54, 57, 65, 67, 68, 70, 76–77, 86-87, 88, 103, 104, 113 bottom, 120 left, 123 right, 128, 130, 131, 133, 134 right, 136 right, 138, 148 top, 151 left, 153; © Mark Lohman: 8, 20, 63, 124, 140; © Karyn Millet: 6–7, 16; © Jacqui Miller/Stocksy: 66 bottom; © Charlotte Moss: 10; © Helen Norman: 42, 50-51, 62, 78, 79, 81, 94, 102, 119, 136 left, 137 left, 150; © Victoria Pearson: 35, 40, 46, 52, 53 left, 55, 60, 80, 96, 112, 113 top, 114, 115, 129, 135 left, 144, 147 right, 148 bottom, 149; © Laura Resen: 17; © Lisa Romerein: 64, 89, 90, 93 right, 95, 151 bottom right; © Annie Schlechter: 24, 25, 58, 105 left, 107, 110, 122; © David Tsay: 19, 28–29, 47, 48, 49, 147 left; © Bjorn Wallender: 41; © Simon Whitmore IPC: 44; © Brian Woodcock: 15, 59 right, 118, 120 right

INDEX

Note: Page references to photos indicate location of photo captions.